THE FREE PRESS
New York London Toronto Sydney Singapore

FAIR PLAY

What Your Child Can Teach You About Economics, Values, and the Meaning of Life

STEVEN E. LANDSBURG

*f*P
THE FREE PRESS
A Division of Simon & Schuster Inc.
1230 Avenue of the Americas
New York, NY 10020

Designed by Carla Bolte

Manufactured in the United States of America

10 9 8 7 6 5 4 3 2 1

Library of Congress Cataloging-in-Publication Data

Landsburg, Steven E.

Fair play: what your child can teach you about economics, values, and the meaning of life/ by Steven E. Landsburg.

p. cm.

Includes bibliographical references.

1. Economics—Moral and ethical aspects. 2. Economics—Study and teaching (Elementary)—Case studies. 3. Concepts in children—Case studies. 4. United States—Economic conditions—1993– I. Title.

HB72.L36 1997

330—dc21

97–35813

CIP

ISBN 0–684–82755–7

CONTENTS

Acknowledgments

The ideas in this book were forged, refined, and polished by fire. The fire was ignited by my colleagues in the Lunch Group, who strive daily, over sandwiches and coffee, to illuminate every aspect of the human condition. Almost always there are sparks. Often there is a flash of insight. Occasionally there is a conflagration.

Our ambition is to understand the world, both as it is and as it ought to be. Each day, one or more of us offers an idea for the group's consideration. Each offering is subjected to criticism so intense and so precisely focused that the idea must either be reduced to ashes or purified and hardened.

Every idea in this book has been tested in the crucible of the lunchtable, and—in my possibly controversial opinion—survived. A dozen times as many were consumed by the flames. Let me explain why that process matters.

Economists believe a lot of things that strike ordinary thoughtful people as self-evidently false. (More disturbingly, economists know to be false a lot of things that strike ordinary thoughtful people as self-evidently true.) It is therefore important to emphasize that we don't just make this stuff up as we go along. Economics is a serious discipline, with reasonably precise standards of logic and evidence. In much of my earlier writing, I've tried to explain what those standards are, and to demonstrate how we apply them to reach conclusions that are sometimes startling.

In my earlier book, *The Armchair Economist,* and in my magazine columns, I have argued that increased promiscuity can retard the spread of AIDS, that charitable people would never give to more than one large charity, and that monopoly theatre owners would not charge high prices for popcorn except under rather special circumstances. Those conclusions might appear implausible, but they all meet the ultimate test of good economic reasoning: Every one of them can be translated into pure mathematics, whereupon it can be verified that the conclusions follow inevitably from the (clearly stated) assumptions. No discourse about economics should be taken seriously unless it meets that test.

This book contains a lot of discourse about economics, and by the standard I've just established, all of it deserves to be taken seriously. I am sure of that because I've performed the mathematical translations myself, as I do whenever I write about economic issues. I am therefore certain that those parts of the book which concern themselves with pure economics are correct, even when they are contrary to what I might have guessed before I calculated.

But this book also contains a lot of discourse about things that are not strictly economics—things of more fundamental importance, like fairness, and justice, and tolerance, and responsibility. That discourse is not entirely susceptible to mathematical verification. Thus my faith in its correctness—and I have considerable faith—must be based on some other powerful discipline. Without that basis, my thoughts on fairness and justice would be no more appropriate for presentation to a general audience than a list of my favorite movies.

The discipline I have come to rely on is the discipline of the lunchtable, where successful ideas must be internally consistent, compatible (in logic and in spirit) with established principles, and applicable in a multitude of hypothetical scenarios—and where every possible failure to meet those criteria is honestly acknowledged and explored. That discipline is less precise than pure mathematics, and I am accordingly less certain of my conclusions about fairness than of my conclusions about economics. But as far as I am aware, it is the best discipline available.

I did not invent all the ideas in this book. But even if I had, I wouldn't have written about them without first subjecting them to the level of scrutiny that—in my experience—only the Lunch Group can provide. Among those who have been particularly helpful are John Boyd, James Kahn, and Alan Stockman, all of whom have provided me with extensive comments both during and after lunch. I am immensely grateful to them. I am grateful too for the helpful comments of Lauren Feinstone, who has stopped coming to lunch but is with us in spirit.

One of the many great things about the Lunch Group is that no dominant figure has ever emerged—the depth of thought and intellectual ardor are uniformly high, and few conclusions are reached without significant contributions from every member. But for the particular issues that are addressed in this book, I owe an exceptionally large debt to Mark Bils. Mark brings to the table an unshakable conviction that fairness is fundamentally important; an insistence that intellectual inquiry can reveal important truths about how we should behave; an eye for the surprising, apt and fruitful analogy that was invisible until Mark revealed it and impossible to ignore thereafter; and an instinct for the kind of irony that demands reconsideration of everything you thought you knew. Through his insistence that fairness could not mean one thing on the playground and another in the marketplace, Mark was the direct inspiration for this book.

Parts of this book have been expanded from my columns in *Forbes* and *Slate.* Those that appeared in *Slate* have benefited from intelligent and sensitive editing, for which I humbly thank Michael Kinsley and Jack Shafer. I am grateful also for the patience, encouragement, and good sense of Bruce Nichols, my editor at the Free Press.

My final acknowledgment is to the staff of Barnes and Noble in Pittsford, New York, where I spend several hours a day working on my laptop computer. They've made me feel warmly welcome, and I hope I can repay them by helping them sell a lot of books.

1

The Economist as Parent and the Parent as Economist

HUNGER AND FATIGUE MAKE ME CRANKY. Food and sleep cheer me up. Somehow I reached adulthood without fully recognizing these truths. I knew them in the way that I knew Aaron Burr was the third Vice President of the United States, but I didn't know them in the way that I know not to step in front of oncoming traffic. They weren't built into my instincts.

With parenthood came wisdom. You can't live with a toddler and fail to discover the palliative benefits of a meal or a nap. Observing those responses in my child, I discovered them in myself. It's helped me to take better care of both of us.

My daughter Cayley, now aged nine and the apple of her father's eye, strove from infancy to focus my attention on certain principles of applied economics, beginning with the importance of material comforts. Cayley and I have been teaching economics to each other ever since.

I also teach economics in another guise, as a professor at a university. Professors and parents have a lot in common. A good professor, like a good parent, is there to teach, to learn, and, in the best of circumstances, to rejoice as his students surpass him.

If you're a parent, then you're an economics teacher. Economics is about facing difficult choices: earning income versus enjoying leisure, splurging today versus saving for tomorrow; developing new skills versus exploiting the skills you've got; searching for the perfect job (or the perfect marriage partner) versus settling for the one that's available. I want my students to think hard about those choices; I want my daughter to think hard about them too.

One of the great lessons of economics is that there is no single best way to resolve such choices; everything depends on circumstances; what's right for you can be wrong for your neighbor. Economics is the science of tolerance. Good economics professors teach their students that people can live very differently than you do without being either foolish or evil. Good parents teach their children the same thing.

Economics breeds not just tolerance but compassion. The economist's method is to observe behavior closely, the better to understand other people's goals and other people's difficulties. That kind of understanding is the basis of all compassion.

I teach a freshman honors seminar in economics. On the first day of class, I ask my students to tell me why today's grocery shoppers demand larger carts than their parents did thirty years ago. Here are some of the better answers: Today's working women can't shop every week the way their mothers did; they (or their husbands) must stock up more on each infrequent trip. Or: Today's working women can't cook dinner for the entire family as their mothers did; instead they buy enough food so that mom, dad, and the kids can all fend for themselves. Or: Today's wealthier families serve a greater variety of dishes at each meal. Or: Today's wealthier shoppers are willing to pay higher grocery prices for luxuries like wide aisles and the carts those aisles can accommodate. Or: Today's larger houses provide more storage space in the pantry. Or: Today's ubiquitous ATM machines mean that shoppers are no longer constrained by their unwillingness to carry lots of cash.

If things go well, students challenge each others' answers in insightful ways. One student says that today's shoppers buy more because advertising techniques have become more effective. Another objects that with a given income, shoppers who buy more of one product must necessarily buy less of another.

The point of the exercise is not to understand shopping carts; it's to understand the technique of understanding. To succeed at this game, students must be sensitive to the problems of families very unlike their own. Learning to see the world through someone else's eyes is an essential part of economic training; it's also an essential part of growing up.

There are a lot of good questions to practice on. Next year I think I'll ask my students why two-earner families generally save less than one-earner families with identical incomes. Is it because the two-earner family hires a housekeeper? Is it because working mothers care less about their children's future than stay-at-home mothers do? Is it because working mothers provide such good role models that their children can make it on their own without a large inheritance?

Or else I'll ask why, in every culture, men are far more likely than women to commit suicide. Is it because women feel a greater obligation to continue caring for their offspring? Or is it because women live longer, and can therefore look forward to surviving the spouse who is making life unbearable?

Teaching this stuff is a lot like parenting, really. When my daughter comes home in distress because she thinks she's been slighted in the schoolyard, I can help by encouraging her to imagine events through the other kids' eyes. There's a technique to that kind of imagination. You make a guess; you ask if it seems plausible; you check whether it's consistent with all the evidence; you refine your guess. That's exactly how a good economics student thinks about shopping carts.

Economics is about more than just individual choices. It's also about social choices: rewarding initiative versus promoting equality; preserving freedom versus preserving order; providing opportunities for the masses versus providing a safety net for the least fortunate. In other words, we want to ask: What is right? What is just? What is fair? My daughter is keenly interested in the same questions, more concretely posed: Is her allowance an entitlement or a reward for a clean room? Should she be free to ignore her parents' advice and wear a summer jacket on a winter day? Should she and her friends choose a video that most of them love or a video that none of them hates? Every time a child cries "That's not fair!", a parent is forced to confront some issue of economic justice.

I am bilingual. In the classroom, I speak the language of graphs and equations; in the living room I speak the language of dreams and imagination and the drying of tears. In the classroom I talk abstractly about the advantages of writing an enforceable contract; in the living room I talk concretely about why Cayley's friend Jessica doesn't like her to change the rules of checkers in the middle of a game. In the classroom I talk about the general problem of delineating property rights; in the living room I talk about the specific moral issues raised when one child lays claim to a quarter of the communal sandbox. Being bilingual doesn't mean you have twice as much to talk about; it means only that you get to talk about the same things twice.

But here's something odd: Sometimes issues that seem murky and difficult in the language of the classroom become clear and simple in the language of the living room, and sometimes the reverse is true. This suggests that parents and economists have a lot to teach each other.

That's what this book is about. It's a patchwork of essays about issues—basic human issues like fairness and justice and responsibility—that both parents and economists are forced to confront. It's about principles of right and wrong which are obvious to every parent, but must be taught to wayward children and wayward economists. It's about techniques of understanding. It's about teaching economics, and using ideas from economics to teach tolerance and compassion and intellectual rigor. It's about using economics to understand the family, and using the structure of the family to illuminate issues in economics.

Every now and then, an insightful college student challenges a professor and turns out to be right. To a conscientious professor, that's the most joyful experience you can have in a classroom. Parents—at least the kind of parents who encourage the lively exchange of ideas among family members—have ample opportunity to feel the same kind of joy. So do opinionated authors, if their readers are attentive. The arguments in this book are the product of sustained and careful thought, and they seem to me to be right. But when they're wrong, I hope that in the spirit of the classroom and the family dinner table, you'll let me know.

2

The Lessons of the Playground

I AM BLESSED WITH A CHILD SO PRECOCIOUS that at age five, when she was watching television and heard newly elected President Bill Clinton announce his intention to increase the income tax, she immediately burst into tears. There never was a prouder father.

The tax package came wrapped in the usual rhetoric: "The rich have too much and the poor have too little"; "They have more than they deserve," "It's only fair," and so forth, *ad tedium*.

From the fact that politicians supply such rhetoric, I infer that there are voters who demand it. Probably that's because it helps them feel less guilty about living by the sweat of their neighbors' brows. Better to pretend your neighbor deserves to be exploited than to admit you're just being acquisitive.

The key word here, though, is "pretend." The fact of the matter is that nobody *really* believes the rhetoric of redistribution. You can use that rhetoric to fool some of the people some of the time, and they might appreciate being fooled. But nobody believes it all of the time, and deep down nobody believes it even some of the time. Nobody even comes close to believing it deep down.

How do I know this? I know it because I have a daughter, and I take my daughter to the playground, and I listen to what the other parents tell their children. In my considerable experience, I have never, ever, heard a parent say to a child that it's okay to forcibly take toys away from other children who have more toys than you do. Nor have I ever heard a parent tell a child that if one kid has more toys than the others, then it's okay for those others to form a "government" and *vote* to take those toys away.

We do, of course, encourage sharing, and we try to make our children feel ashamed when they are very selfish. But at the same time, we tell them that if another child is being selfish, you must cope with that in some way short of forcible expropriation. You can cajole, you can bargain, you can ostracize, but you cannot simply steal. Moreover, there is no such thing as a legitimate government with the moral authority to do your stealing for you. No constitutional convention or democratic process or any other institution of any sort can create a government with that moral authority, because there is simply no such thing.

These are not morally complex issues, no matter how much we try to pretend otherwise. Politicians and commentators make their livings by encouraging that pretense, but when we talk to our children the pretense falls away.

No adult has any difficulty distinguishing between good and bad behavior on the playground.

The lessons we teach our children reveal the truth that is in our hearts. If you want to know what a politician or a commentator really believes, look not to his speeches or his columns, but to the advice he gives his children. If you want to know whether a politician is behaving well or badly, ask how his behavior would be received in your family room.

A few years ago, I took my daughter Cayley and her friend Alix to dinner; they must have been six years old. For dessert, each had a choice of ice cream now or bubble gum later. Alix chose the ice cream; Cayley chose the bubble gum. (Money-saving tip for new parents: Start early and convince your kids that bubble gum is a dessert.)

After Alix had finished her ice cream, we went off to buy Cayley's gum. Cayley got her gum, Alix got nothing, and Alix cried foul. To any adult outsider, it would have been clear that Alix had no case. She'd been given the same choices as Cayley had and had taken her rewards up front.

The same issues arise in adult life. Paul and Peter face the same range of opportunities in their youth. Paul chooses the easy life, working forty hours a week for a guaranteed wage. Peter devotes his youth to creating a new enterprise, working around the clock for risky rewards. Then, in middle age, when Peter is rich and Paul is not, Paul cries foul and assaults the system that fosters inequality.

I wouldn't want to argue that Peter's choice is intrinsically more admirable than Paul's, any more than I would want to argue that a taste for gum is intrinsically more admirable than a taste for ice cream. But I do want to argue with Paul's reasoning about the *consequences* of that choice. A good test is to ask whether any adult would take it seriously in a dispute between first graders. Paul's griping fails that test.

And what about differences in income that result not from choice but from pure chance? Once again, look to what you tell your children. If you've ever served cake to more than once child at a time, you've heard the refrain "No fair—my piece is smaller." And if you were feeling very patient at the time, you might have tried to explain that a child who can enjoy his cake without regard for what's on his sister's plate can expect a lot more happiness in life than a child who is constantly distracted by the need to make comparisons. Because we want our children to be happy, we tell them that when somebody gives you a piece of cake, you have occasion to rejoice, and that if another child has more, you might remember that the world is also full of children who have less. Remember that lesson the next time your coworker gets an undeserved promotion.

The disconnect between the standards adults impose on themselves, and the standards they impose on their children, is rarely to the adults' credit. If you live in the average American household, the Corporation for Public Broadcasting lifts about $5 a year from your pocketbook to fund projects like National Public Radio. NPR apologists (adults all) attempt to dismiss that small predation by pointing to others that are much larger: The Navy alone, for example, spends ten times as much for weapons procurement.

Perhaps those apologists are aiming their appeals exclusively at childless voters. What parent could accept an excuse like "Sure, I stole the cookies, but I know another kid who stole a bicycle"?

All parents know a specious argument when they see one. Voters, by contrast, buy into specious arguments all the time. The great paradox is that parents and voters are often the same people. I believe the source of the paradox is that—quite sensibly—we tend to think harder about how and when to discipline our kids than we do about how and when to discipline our congressmen.

My proposal is to save intellectual labor by recognizing that you don't have to think separately about your kids and your congressman. A good rule of thumb is that if your kids aren't allowed to get away with something, neither you nor your congressman should be allowed to get away with it either.

3

What Cayley Knows

NEARLY EVERY ECONOMIST IN AMERICA is appalled by Pat Buchanan's revival of protectionism. So is my daughter Cayley. The difference is that, unlike the economists, Cayley is appalled for the right reasons.

Economists know that trade is the engine of prosperity. From this they deduce—correctly—that a national refusal to trade is a national refusal to prosper. They cite studies showing—again correctly—that to save one American autoworker's $50,000 job through tariffs or import quotas, car buyers collectively pay an extra $150,000 a year through higher prices. They argue—correctly once again—that free trade, like technological progress, might displace some workers but must make Americans wealthier on average.

Those are the arguments I make in my college classroom. My favorite teaching tool is a fable based on a tale told by Professor James Ingram of North Carolina State University.

It's the tale of a brilliant entrepreneur who invented a new technology for turning grain into cars. The entrepreneur built a factory by the sea, surrounded its inner workings with secrecy, and commenced production.

Consumers were thrilled to learn that the new cars were better and cheaper than anything Detroit had to offer. Midwestern farmers were thrilled when the factory ordered vast amounts of grain to feed into its mysterious machinery. There was indeed dismay among those autoworkers who had been trained in the old methods, but there was also a general recognition that technological progress, even when accompanied by growing pains, is on balance a very good thing.

One day an investigative reporter managed to locate a disgruntled employee who revealed the entrepreneur's great secret. The vast factory was hollow. The back wall opened out onto a shipping dock. Grain came in the front door and went out the back, where it was sent to foreign countries in exchange for cars.

The shock of these revelations transformed the entrepreneur from a public hero to a public villain. Riding a wave of popular outrage, Pat Buchanan was swept into the Oval Office.

The moral, of course, is that inexpensive cars are a good thing, and equally a good thing whether we acquire them with technology or by trade. Cutting off trade is exactly like closing the most efficient factories. To support a Buchanan, you must be blind to that fundamental equivalence. The willfully blind are unlikely to prosper.

That's what I tell my students. But it's not what I tell my daughter. Unlike my students, Cayley relies on me for moral guidance. Sure, I could explain to her how trade makes our family richer. But nine-year-olds are quite self-centered enough; it's their concern for others that needs gentle encouragement. So instead of telling Cayley how great it is for our family to save money at the car dealer's, I talk to her about the difference between right and wrong.

She knows a lot about right and wrong already. She is an active trader in the schoolyard markets for decals, trading cards, and milk bottle caps. Sometimes Cayley wants to trade with her classmate Melissa but Melissa prefers to deal with Jennifer, from the other fourth-grade classroom. Cayley knows how disappointing that can be, but she also knows she can't force Melissa to trade with her. More important, she knows it would be wrong to try.

Cayley is too morally advanced even to imagine asking her teacher to intervene and prohibit Melissa from trading with "foreigners." Only a very unpalatable child would attempt such a tactic.

Buchanan sees the U.S. Congress as the great national teacher, maintaining order on the schoolyard, making sure that all the children play the way the teachers' special pets—or special industries—want them to play. My daughter thinks that stinks. She's right.

Protectionism is wrong because it robs individuals of a basic human right: the freedom to choose one's trading partners. The freedom, for example, to buy any car, at any price, from any willing seller.

But protectionism is wrong also for another reason. It's a reason that my daughter understands and Pat Buchanan doesn't, and it sits at the core of what it means to be a decent human being. My daughter knows that all people are created equal, and that nobody's right to prosper should be altered by being born on the wrong side of an imaginary national boundary line. It would never occur to her to care more about an autoworker in Detroit than about an autoworker in Tokyo or Mexico City.

Forget all that stuff about how much it costs American consumers to save the job of an American worker. Suppose Buchanan were right; suppose he *did* have some miracle formula that could save American jobs at zero cost to consumers. His views would still be repugnant, because they start from the presumption that an American worker is more worthy of protection than a foreign worker. What moral foundation could support such an ugly division of humanity?

Buchanan has frequently been accused of racism, and I happen to think he's suffered a lot of bum raps on that score. But there is poetic justice in those bum raps, because his simplistic nationalism is every bit as ugly as racism, and in exactly the same way. Encouraging people to "buy American" is no different in principle from encouraging people to "buy white."

We need to care about others. We need to care about those who are close to us, and we need to care about strangers. But to care more about strangers who happen to be American than about strangers who happen to be Japanese or Mexican is an expression of the basest and most wrong-headed instincts that a person can have. Thank God my nine-year-old knows better.

It was long ago, early in the election year of 1992, when Cayley—then almost five years old—became politically aware. It was a year when every major candidate wanted to increase the size and scope of government. The incumbent

George Bush had just presided over a four-year orgy of federal regulatory expansion; the Democratic front-runner Bill Clinton promised nationalized health care; Bush's primary challenger Pat Buchanan sought to close the borders; and Clinton's primary challenger Paul Tsongas (do you remember Paul Tsongas?) was running on an industrial policy platform that could have been crafted by Mussolini. I mean that seriously, by the way: Senator Tsongas's success in the early primaries was America's closest brush with something like full-fledged fascism since World War II—until the emergence of Ross Perot later in that same dreadful year.

Cayley had a keen sense that her parents found the options less than adequate, and was eager to understand more. One night she sat me down and asked me to explain the issues. I summarized as best I could in language suitable for a five-year-old, while making an honest effort to preserve the spirit of what the candidates were saying. For example, I explained Buchanan's trade policy by telling Cayley that Buchanan does not think people should be allowed to decide for themselves what kind of car to buy.

She went off to think for a few minutes, and returned to announce that she had decided to endorse Buchanan. Her explanation was that "I don't *care* what kind of car we buy."

I could have taken the opportunity to explain the theory of comparative advantage, and in particular the fact that when we have fewer options, cars become more expensive—leaving us less income for other material goods that might matter to a five-year-old. But in addition to being futile, that would have been shirking my parental responsibility for Cayley's moral development. Instead I pointed out that some people *do* care what kind of car they buy, and we should care about other people's liberty as well as our own.

I think that's the moment when my daughter became an expert in international trade. She got the point, and she developed a lasting and clear understanding of a fundamental moral issue that professors of economics frequently refuse to confront.

Those of us who teach for a living know that you never really understand a difficult idea until you've explained it to a student. Those of us who are also parents learn that you never really understand a *simple* idea until you've explained it to a child. There is a subject called "welfare economics," which provides mathematical tools for analyzing policy choices according to various ethical criteria. Those tools are, I believe, indispensable for anyone who wants to think seriously about genuinely subtle issues of economic justice. But those same tools can be used to create illusions of subtlety in cases where the underlying truth is really very straightforward. Such illusions ought to be shattered, and talking to a child is an excellent way to shatter them. You can't dazzle a preschooler with technical wizardry. You have to get down to basics. We *should* care about the rights of people who are different than we are. It really is that simple.

Cayley and I try not to shop at Wal-Mart. We don't always succeed; sometimes we're very eager to buy an item that's not easily available except at Wal-Mart. But when we can, we prefer to shop elsewhere.

That's a conscious echo of Wal-Mart's own well-advertised policies. Signs posted in every aisle boast of the store's efforts not to carry imported goods. Wal-Mart does not always succeed, admit the signs; sometimes they're very eager to carry an item that's not easily available except from abroad. But when Wal-Mart can, it prefers to "buy American—so you can too."

By the time Cayley was old enough to read those signs, she was old enough to know that people who want you to care about the race or religion or sex or national origin of your trading partners are bad people. Even Wal-Mart managers are likely to have learned that truth in childhood. Adults who want to believe otherwise must resort to extremes of sophistry that are not accessible to elementary schoolers.

Such sophistry is readily available; if it weren't, Wal-Mart would be out of business. As would Senator Dianne Feinstein of California. Senator Feinstein opposes "cruel and inhumane" cuts in public health and education benefits for illegal immigrants, but supports stricter border controls to prevent illegals from entering the country in the first place. Only an extraordinary intellectual contortionist could justify such bald hypocrisy. Either Senator Feinstein cares about Mexicans or she doesn't. If she doesn't care about them, what's all this about inhumanity? If she does care, how can she justify confining those Mexicans to Mexico?

Like the management of Wal-Mart, the Senator appears to subscribe to some bizarre notion that we should care more about total strangers who happen to reside in the United States than about total strangers who happen to reside elsewhere, and that if we can force those strangers to stay on one side of an imaginary line then we need have no concern for their welfare. I cannot imagine any reasonable moral principle that would justify such a notion.

But of course Senator Feinstein is not motivated by any moral principle at all; her only goal is to advance the material interests of those Californians—mostly Anglo—who already have the extraordinary good fortune to be citizens of the United States of America. She believes those citizens will enjoy beneficial spillover effects from the health and education of their nearby Mexican neighbors, but can safely ignore the health, education, and welfare of Mexicans living a few hundred miles further south.

If Senator Feinstein were, say, a principled libertarian, then she'd favor allowing people to live where they choose. If she were a principled egalitarian, her concern for the relatively fortunate Mexicans who have made it across the border would be dwarfed by her concern for their impoverished former neighbors still stranded on the other side. Only by having no principles at all can she simultaneously demand that we offer more to the fortunate few and less to the unfortunate many.

Okay, so Senator Feinstein serves her constituents without regard to any sense of right and wrong. Perhaps that's all we can expect of a politician (and perhaps it's a good reason to limit the power of all politicians whenever and wherever we can). But her references to the "cruelty" and "inhumanity" of those who disagree with her suggest that she values having a moral smokescreen for her actions. And I'll bet she's got one. If the Senator were offered equal space on this page, she'd surely have no trouble concocting some superficially plausible way of reconciling her contradictory views. But I don't think my daughter would buy it.

Go ahead and try it with the child of your choice. Explain that there is a U.S. senator who believes that relatively rich foreigners who happen to live in America should receive additional benefits while relatively poor foreigners who happen to live in Mexico should be forgotten. In economics classrooms we are able to analyze such proposals with dead seriousness because we forget that they are ludicrous to the core. The advantage of explaining them to children is that, in order to be understood, you've got to strip away the surrounding verbiage and display the underlying assumptions with devastating clarity.

The textbook case for free immigration is very like the textbook case for free trade: We account for costs and benefits to all Americans and argue that the benefits must exceed the costs. In the case of immigration, the costs are borne by American workers (who are hurt by falling wages) and the benefits are reaped by American capitalists (who profit from those same falling wages). A competent economics student can represent both the costs and the benefits as areas on a graph, and can use some elementary geometry to conclude that the area representing benefits is the larger one.

The story underlying the geometry is this: When the worker earns a dollar less, the capitalist must earn a dollar more. So far, the benefits and costs exactly balance. But capitalists enjoy an additional benefit: A fall in wages allows them to profitably expand their operations. Thus capitalists' gains exceed workers' losses.[1]

---

1. Journalists seem to think that the costs of foreign competition can be measured by the number of Americans who leave their jobs as a result. That's pretty much the opposite of the truth. Those Americans who leave their jobs rather than take wage cuts to match the new competitors are presumably those Americans who cared the least about their jobs in the first place. The big losers are those Americans who value their jobs highly enough to keep them and absorb the full impact of the wage cut.

If you accept cost-benefit analysis as a reasonable guide to policy (and if you believe the textbook analysis has captured all the relevant costs and benefits) then we have here an argument for free immigration. Most economists—including me—do believe that cost-benefit analyses are relevant to policy, and most economics textbooks contain some (qualified) defense of that relevance. Typically, the defense appeals partly to naked self-interest ("if U.S. policymakers are consistently guided by cost-benefit analysis, then in the long run most Americans—probably including yourself—will win more than they lose") and partly to ethical principles ("cost-benefit analysis treats everybody equally; a cost is a cost, no matter who bears it").

The appeal to self-interest I can understand, but the appeal to ethical principles makes no sense. For in fact this particular cost-benefit analysis does *not* treat everybody equally; it treats all *Americans* equally—while completely ignoring the interests of those who are not yet Americans but would like to be.

As it happens, admitting that foreigners are human would only strengthen the argument's conclusion, so in that sense no harm is done by pretending otherwise. The pretense may even serve some rhetorical value; we ostentatiously ignore the most obvious beneficiaries of open borders and can *still* conclude that open borders are a good thing! It's rather like winning a chess match after you've spotted your opponent a queen.

As it also happens, there might be an economic argument for assuming the gains to new immigrants are negligible anyway. The argument goes like this: If sufficiently many

Mexicans enter the United States, they'll drive American wages and working conditions down to the Mexican level, in which case they themselves will have gained exactly nothing. So the gains we're "ignoring" never had a chance to materialize in the first place, and nothing is lost by omitting them from the analysis.

But this argument subtly assumes that all Mexicans are identical; otherwise some would have special skills or preferences that allow them to prosper specifically in the United States even when conditions are superficially the same in both countries. An analogous assumption about Americans—that all American workers are identical—would lead to the conclusion that wages are *already* bid down to the level where employed and unemployed Americans are equally happy, and thus no American could be harmed by losing his job to foreign competition.

All of this is appropriate grist for the classroom, where I would welcome multiple rounds of point and counterpoint. All of it is important. And all of it is far beyond the grasp of any child (and of many adults). Silly folk songs notwithstanding, untutored youth is no great repository of wisdom.

That means that serious insights about issues like trade and immigration can come only from thoughtful adults. But sometimes an adult can be made more thoughtful through conversation with a child. The points and counterpoints all matter, but this matters too: There's no comfortable way to tell a ten-year-old that you'd prefer not to think about the problems of distant Mexicans.

Cayley, aged three, cuddled up with her dad to watch the animated Mousekewitz family of *An American Tail* as they fled from oppressive Old World cats to a promise of freedom across the sea. She gripped my hand in anticipation as the Statue of Liberty loomed in the distance. She sighed with relief as the Mouskewitzes disembarked. But then disaster struck. Feivel Mousekewitz was pressed into service in a sweatshop, chained to a sewing machine. First horrified, then indignant, Cayley placed her hands firmly on her hips and declared "This is not America!"

She was right, of course. It wasn't America, or at best it was only a small and unrepresentative piece of America. Cayley didn't know that Feivel's children would own their own tailor shops, and that his grandchildren would build great commercial empires, or cure diseases, or expand the limits of human knowledge. She didn't know that America would keep its promise to Feivel Mousekewitz and be repaid for it many times over. She knew only that she wanted Feivel to be happy. Not bad for a three-year-old.

The landmark that symbolized Feivel's freedom bears the words: "Give me your tired, your poor, your huddled masses yearning to breathe free, the wretched refuse of your teeming shore; send these, the homeless, tempest-tossed, to me: I lift my lamp beside the golden door." I'm not sure how well Cayley understands those words, but I know she understands the sentiment behind them.

4

Authority

BY THE TIME MY DAUGHTER WAS IN FIRST grade, she knew more than the average six-year-old about the diversity of adult opinion. Her teachers—then as now—extolled the virtues of going to the library; Cayley has long known that her father disapproves of libraries, on the grounds that any book worth reading is a book worth owning. Her teachers taught her to recognize the constellations; but the locations of the stars are merely facts, and Cayley knows too that in her father's opinion there is nothing less interesting than a fact unilluminated by a theory. I make a point of calling her attention to such little differences, to help her avoid the trap of believing there is some monolithic body of adult opinion she is expected to master.

A healthy skepticism—or even an active disrespect for authority—is a public school child's best defense against teachers who are patsies for the two great contemporary hysterias: environmentalism and the War on Drugs. The antidrug propaganda begins in early elementary school, but the environmental propaganda begins even sooner: By the time Cayley was four years old, she had come briefly under the sway of a maniacal preschool teacher who drilled her charges to chant the slogan "with privilege comes responsibility," along with elaborations like "with the privilege of living on this planet comes the responsibility to care for it."

Thus the Declaration of Independence—with its quaint notion that life on this planet is an inalienable right—is replaced in the classroom by a Declaration of *Inter*dependence, holding as self-evident the proposition that our rights are constricted by so many obligations to each other (or, depending on your denomination, to all creatures great and small, or to the universe itself) that they are no longer rights at all, but merely "privileges," to be granted or revoked at the whim of the environmentalist gods. And what high priest or priestess can reveal the will of those gods? The teacher, of course.

The cult of environmentalism demands that children abandon all independent thought about the nature of rights and obligations, replacing it with mindless subservience to the value judgments of their teachers.

It wouldn't be difficult for teachers to address environmental issues in a refreshingly different way—as invitations to critical thought. I believe, for example, that my child is old enough to think sensibly about the issue of whether to leave the water running while she brushes her teeth. When she lets water run down the drain, she denies other people the use of that water. The value of that use, to a very good approximation, is measured by the *price* of the water.

Cayley, now aged nine, is capable—with a little assistance in the form of leading questions—of estimating how much water escapes during a toothbrushing session, the value of that water, and whether that value is or is not high enough to justify the effort of turning the faucets off and on. That's a good exercise in estimation and a good exercise in arithmetic. It's also a great way for her to discover the true miracle of the marketplace: As long as Cayley cares about her own family's water bill, she will *automatically* account for the interests of everyone else who might be interested in using that water.

But Cayley's teachers have not wanted her to think clearly about such issues, perhaps out of fear that clear thought can become a habit, and habitual clear thinkers are not good candidates for subservience. Instead, those teachers have pronounced from on high that because water is valuable to others, we should be exceptionally frugal with it. In an inquisitive child, this raises the question: With exactly *which* valuable resources are we obligated to be exceptionally frugal? A child who is observant as well as inquisitive will quickly recognize that "*all* valuable resources" is not the teacher's preferred answer. For example, teachers rarely argue that "because building supplies are valuable to others, we ought to build fewer schools"; even more rarely do they argue that "because skilled workers are valuable in industry, we ought to have fewer teachers."

Where is the pattern, then? What general rule compels us to conserve water but not to conserve on resources devoted to education? The blunt truth is that there *is* no pattern, and the general rule is simply this: Only the teacher can tell you which resources should be conserved. The whole exercise is not about toothbrushing; it is about authority.

That lesson is reinforced again and again. My daughter was taught to rinse and reuse her paper cup so she doesn't waste paper. She was never taught to discard the cup so she doesn't waste time and effort. Who decided that the paper in the cup mattered more than her time and effort? The teacher. On what grounds? None whatsoever, other than that the teacher is always right.

Here's how I'd like to see a teacher handle the drinking cup issue: Give each student a small amount of cash (or play money), to be used for purchasing paper cups or other trinkets over the course of the year. Students who wash and reuse their cups will have more left over to spend on beads and marbles. Students who prefer to buy a new cup each day can start recess thirty seconds earlier while their more frugal classmates are standing in line to wash their cups.

That system could be used to generate some lively class discussion about the pros and cons of the two strategies. Children would be forced to think about trade-offs. Best of all, they might even discover the most important truth of all, which is that there *is* no single best strategy; that some students care more about marbles while others care more about playtime, and *that's okay.* A disagreement about how to allocate one's limited resources is not an appropriate occasion for moral condemnation.

But instead, teachers convey exactly the wrong message: that there is only one right choice, and it cannot be discovered through any process resembling reason. Teachers do this partly because it enhances their own authority and partly because it's easier for a not-terribly-intelligent teacher to demand rote memorization than to guide students through the shoals of logical thought.

That's why American junior high school kids can tell you exactly how fast the Amazon rain forest is shrinking, but have absolutely no framework for thinking about whether it's shrinking too fast or not fast enough. It's easy for a teacher to write a number on a blackboard (the rain forest is shrinking by such-and-such a number of square miles per year) and demand that students memorize that mere fact, unilluminated by any theory. It's much harder to get students to think sensibly about the alternative uses of that land, and the difficult issue of how to weigh those alternatives against each other. Because it's so much harder, most teachers don't bother.

When my daughter had just started fourth grade, I told her how the pioneers cleared the forests of nineteenth century Ohio for agriculture, and her first question was "Didn't they know that trees make oxygen?" I pointed out that people need food as well as oxygen. She was unimpressed. To her, trees were by nature more important than farmland; the idea that there might be some optimal balance between the two was foreign to everything she'd been taught in school. Of course, each nine-year-old has her own idiosyncratic misconceptions, and perhaps Cayley was the only student in her class who had fallen into this one. So I won't go so far as to put all the blame on her teachers. But Cayley's mistake *was* precisely the kind of misconception which frequently, and inappropriately, gets reinforced in the classroom.

After environmentalism, the main area where Cayley requires periodic deprogramming is in her attitude toward drugs. Her teachers tell her that no experiment, no learning experience, no pure hedonistic pleasure, is worth even the slightest risk in this arena. That's bad economics. I hope never to have an adolescent daughter as fearful of life's possibilities as Cayley's teachers would like her to be.

Cayley was a Grateful Dead fan before she started second grade. (This was over a year before the death of Jerry Garcia.) All through that year, she begged me to take her to a Dead concert; I now regret terribly that we never got around to it. Once I teased her that "if you want to go to a Grateful Dead concert, you have to take a lot of drugs." Cayley put hands on hips, stared me down sternly and said "Dad! The *Grateful Dead* would not want you to take *drugs.*"

Maybe that's charming naiveté, or maybe its the result of heavy indoctrination in the belief that there has never been a "good guy" who uses drugs. But I do point out to Cayley that her Dad drinks a lot of caffeine, and that caffeine is a drug, and that I think it would be a lot harder to write books without it. I also tell her that a lot of other drugs are far more dangerous than caffeine, and that some can kill you. But then I also tell her that a *lot* of things can kill you, and not all of them are bad ideas.

I suspect that parents systematically encourage children to err on the side of caution, for this reason: When a child engages in risky behavior, the parent shares more in the costs than in the benefits. If my daughter climbs out on the edge of a cliff and falls off, it will be as horrible for me as it is for her. If she climbs out on the edge of a cliff and feels exhilaration, it will be a far more glorious experience for her than it is for me. That means that, weighing costs against benefits, she should probably climb out on more cliffs than I want her to. There is a moral here for drug policy.

Hillary Clinton believes that it takes a village—and by extension, a great federal bureaucracy—to raise a child. Republicans scoff, emphasizing that it takes not a village but a traditional family—while at the same time criticizing the Clinton administration for doing too *little* to keep kids off drugs; apparently those Republicans believe that it takes not a village but a police state. In the traditional family as I remember it, drug education was supplied by the parents, not the government. At any rate, I wish they'd all lay off my daughter. Education about risks is one thing; telling kids that there's a single "right" response to those risks is something different and more sinister.

This brings us to the relationship between the authority of a teacher and the authority of the government. To think about that relationship, it helps to have a few facts on the table.

First, colleges weed out a *lot* of weak students. According to standard aptitude tests, college graduates are, on average, far brighter than college freshmen; in fact two thirds of all college graduates were in the top half of their freshman classes (as measured by standard aptitude tests). On the other hand, those college graduates who go into teaching are, on average, about exactly as bright as college freshman; among students who become teachers, only half were in the top half of their freshman classes. It's as if the weeding-out process completely bypasses the education majors.

That means that teachers, on average, are no intellectual giants. That might have something to do with why curricula are as they are. There are also darker theories.

Professor John Lott of the University of Pennsylvania has presented evidence that across countries, expenditures on public schooling (as well as expenditures on public broadcasting) are positively correlated with levels of totalitarianism. (That is, by and large, the more totalitarian the country, the more it spends on public schooling.) By contrast, expenditures on public health, and other services with no obvious propaganda value, are *not* positively correlated with totalitarianism. This suggests that public schooling serves a rather unsavory agenda.

You might want to argue that totalitarian regimes tend to take over *every* aspect of public life, so it's not surprising that they spend a lot on public schools. That theory founders, however, when you realize that it makes the (false) prediction that totalitarian regimes spend a lot on public health as well.

Why, indeed, do we have public schools at all? There are advantages to having an educated public, and there are at least arguments to the effect that the private sector will undersupply education. But that's an argument for government subsidies or vouchers; it's not an argument for the government to actually run the schools. The reason the government wants to run schools is so that it can control what is taught. I hope that makes people uncomfortable.

There's no way to combat each and every thing your child learns in school, so instead I work on instilling a healthy general skepticism. From time to time, Cayley and I have little talks about how teachers are often wrong. When I encourage my daughter to resist her teachers' authority, I am simultaneously pursuing two separate aspects of her economic education. First, I am trying to give her the strength to resist a lot of the *bad* economics that her teachers try to foist on her, for example in the realms of the enviroment and drug use. But second, I am directly reinforcing one of the central lessons of economics: that authority is very often a bad thing.

I want to pursue that thought, but first I'll ask you to bear with a digression. I want to point out that the extent to which *adults* defer to authority is an extraordinary and mysterious thing: 535 members of the United States Congress vote to pass a measure, and, for the most part, 260 million Americans choose to obey it. Why does that happen? What strange force do these guys exert?

The naive answer is that we obey them because they've got the guns, but that's really not true. The military and the police have the guns, not the Congress. If the rest of us take orders from the police because the police have a monopoly on physical force, then why do the police take orders from Bill Clinton and Trent Lott?

It's one of those questions a child might ask, but, as far as I know, no adult can answer. That suggests that it's a question worth thinking about. I am aware of only three or four attempts to do that. The attempt with which I am most familiar is that of my colleague James Kahn. Of course when I say that Kahn is one of only a handful of people ever to think about this issue, I am using the word "think" to mean what it ought to mean in the context of social issues, namely "build an economic model."

What Kahn does is to posit a population of individuals who must choose between productive activities and stealing from each other. Thieves discourage productive activities, and fail to account for the fact that this has negative consequences for *other* thieves. That means that each thief would be willing to cut back on his thievery in exchange for his competitors' agreement to do the same. At the same time, producers can allocate resources to security, but they fail to account for the benefits they confer on their neighbors by discouraging people from becoming criminals. Thus each producer would be willing to take additional security measures in exchange for his neighbors' agreement to do the same. So there are a lot of mutually beneficial agreements that would work well if only they could be enforced.

In such a world, criminals might do well to join forces, forming a monopoly crime syndicate that restrains its members from overexploiting the productive sector. Kahn envisions an enforcement mechanism that involves the transfer of weaponry from decentralized bands of criminals to the central syndicate, which then improves the social outcome by enforcing an agreement that no thief should steal an excessive amount.

This model seems to me to be an admirable first attempt to think seriously about the way societies evolve out of Hobbesian states of nature into organized hierarchies with recognized authority figures. It is, however, far too abstract and stylized to capture the details of the world in which we live. It fails, for example to predict that the central crime syndicate will consist of 535 individuals in a bicameral organization. To construct a model that detailed is a topic for further research.

A more accessible, and more important, topic for further research is the relative desirability of an unchallenged monopoly syndicate as opposed to, say, a monopolist facing constant threats from a competitive fringe. In other words: If you must have your property plundered by gangs of thieves, do you prefer a single gang that understands about geese and golden eggs, or do you prefer several gangs whose turf wars distract part of their attention? Kahn's model in its present form does not suffice to answer this question, and I am not aware of any model that does.

What this means in practice is that when the Justice Department prosecutes an organized crime family, I'm not sure which side to root for. Violent urban gangs are scary things. So are police forces who face no competition in the market for extortion. I don't know which is worse. I do know that there is an issue here worth worrying about. The best argument I've ever seen against gun control was on a bumper sticker that said "When guns are outlawed, only the police will have guns."

My daughter's teachers believe that it is not important to think deeply about social issues. They teach her that the police are good and gangsters are bad. But that's the conclusion of an argument that's never been made, and by jumping to the conclusion the teachers deny the importance of argument generally.

It really is a lesson of economics that things are not always as they seem, and that one ought not jump to conclusions in the absence of clear assumptions and close reasoning. So in urging my daughter to reject her teachers' prejudices, I think that I am giving her a head start in economics.

I remember my own first grade teacher and how stirring she found the words of John F. Kennedy, as he took the reins of the country and challenged his fellow citizens to—and here I paraphrase only slightly—"Ask not what I can do for you; ask what you can do for me." Ever since, I've been alert to pro-government prejudice among teachers and other opinion leaders. Let me give you some examples of how widespread these prejudices are.

I'll begin with a prejudice that was articulated most clearly by former Senator Paul Tsongas, the man whose New Hampshire primary victory almost kept Bill Clinton out of the White House. Senator Tsongas opposed the death penalty, except when the victim is a "representative of society" such as a political candidate or a policeman. It was Jim Kahn who pointed out to me that the Senator was apparently incapable of distinguishing between a representative of *society* and a representative of the *government.* By what insane calculation is a congressional candidate more representative of *society* than an entrepreneur, a corporate director, or a taxicab driver? Yet nobody in the media ever called Tsongas on this point. It went right by them. The elevation of government officials above the rest of us is so ingrained that we don't even notice it any more. And this episode is no mere footnote to ancient political history; something like the Tsongas position on capital punishment is now the law in several states.

Here's another example. Do you remember Zoe Baird? She was President Clinton's first choice for attorney general, disqualified after it was discovered that she had illegally employed a nanny for her children. For this she apologized, and there was much discussion of whether her apology was sufficient. But I heard nobody in the classrooms or the media suggest what seemed to obvious to *me,* namely that Ms. Baird's behavior was a positive *qualification* for the job. The last thing I want is an attorney general who thinks that people should go around blindly obeying laws. I want an attorney general who believes that bad laws are bad and should be ignored. And the fact that not one editorialist took this position is ultimately a failure of their elementary school teachers.

And here's another: When President Clinton proposed a costly crime bill that Republican critics denounced as ineffective and filled with pork, New York's mayor Rudolph Giuliani endorsed the criticism—but he endorsed the crime bill too, after noting that a lot of that pork was destined for Manhattan. The bill might be bad for the country, but it was good for New York, and it was Giuliani's job to look out for New York's interests.

That makes Giuliani the moral equivalent of the thief who justifies his occupation by noting that he's looking out for the interests of his family. "I'm looking out for the people I care about" is no excuse for bad behavior in private life, and it should be no excuse for bad behavior in public life either.

Giuliani, of course, was just doing his job. One could say the same about a professional hitman. The hitman wins little sympathy, but Giuliani gets a free ride. Why the double standard? I suggest that it's because we give too much instinctive respect to elected officials.

A fourth example: In the early 1980s, the Mafia took control of the Concrete Workers Union in New York City and used its clout to levy a 1% tax on every building contract in the city. The scheme was ended by the combined efforts of federal, state, and local authorities, each of whom levied (and continues to levy) taxes far in excess of 1%. In this instance, it's clear that of the two taxing authorities—the Mafia and the government—the government was by far the more rapacious. It might well have been better for the building industry if the Mafia had successfully driven out the government than if the government had successfully driven out the Mafia. But newspapers dutifully reported the confrontation as a battle between the good guys and the bad guys. It could have been more accurately characterized as a turf war between two leeches.

In fact, this is an excellent example of the kind of question that is raised by Jim Kahn's research, which I referred to earlier. The Mafia and the government jointly overtax the building industry to the point where a lot of construction projects are abandoned. By eliminating the Mafia, the government is able to ease the burden on construction companies and thereby increase its own share of the take. That sounds like a win for both the government and the construction companies. But at the same time, the government, having eliminated its rival, can now bring more resources to bear on tax collection. So the consolidation of power by a monopoly tax collector is at best a mixed blessing for the productive sector of the economy.

A fifth, and more recent, example: At the 1996 Republican Convention, Jack Kemp—with a straight face—called for bolting the "back door" to illegal immigration so that we can open wide the front door and welcome immigrants to enter legally. But why would anybody bolt the back door to keep out welcome company? Why should immigrants be any more or less welcome at one door than at the other? When a moving van arrives in the Kemp neighborhood, must Mr. Kemp first check whether the van came up the street or down the street before he can decide whether to welcome his new neighbors or to put up a higher fence? No, it's not the means of arrival that Kemp was obsessing on; it's the presence or absence of a government stamp of approval. So let me rework the question: When that moving van arrives, do the Kemps turn to some government agency for guidance on how to treat their new neighbors? The answer is certainly no, so why does it change to yes if the new neighbors happen to come from another country? I submit that there is no good answer to that question. I can understand wanting to welcome people no matter how they get here. I can understand—though with greater difficulty—wanting to turn people *away* no matter how they get here. But to turn to the government for advice on who to welcome and who to reject—that is a position that is not consistent with any principle whatsoever. It is consistent only with blind exaltation of government, and the fact that Kemp was taken seriously illustrates how widespread that blind exaltation must be.

A final example, from personal experience. A few years ago I published a book called *The Armchair Economist* in which I argued that bipartisanship in Congress should be treated as a violation of antitrust law. We don't allow the presidents of United and American Airlines to conspire against the public; why should we allow the leaders of the Democratic and Republican parties to conspire? I got a note back from a copy editor asking whether there wasn't actually a key difference, in the sense that the airline presidents are conspiring to *break* laws, while the politicians are conspiring to *make* laws. I wrote back, asking if he had any historical evidence as to which of these activities was more likely to be harmful. My *guess* is that making laws is on average worse than breaking them. The fact that this possibility never occurred to my editor is another instance of the kind of indoctrination I am talking about.

If you want to combat this stuff, you take the opportunities that come your way. For example, when your three-year-old starts asking about your radar detector, you have a limited number of options. Total honesty requires explaining that the sole purpose of a radar detector is to facilitate breaking the law. Partial honesty can be served by hiding the radar detector.

My colleague Alan Stockman faced this dilemma when his oldest daughter Gwendolyn turned three and curious. Alan opted for the hide-the-detector strategy, lest Gwendolyn get the idea that all rules are made to be broken. The truth, of course, is that some rules are made to be broken and others are not, but philosophers as subtle as Saint Thomas Aquinas have grappled with the question of where to draw the line. For Aquinas the key criterion was conformity with natural law, which is all well and good for a sophisticated adult, but Alan didn't think his three-year-old was quite prepared to grasp the concept of a natural speed limit.

So to maintain his daughter's respect for the rule of law, Alan lived without a radar detector for a few years. There would be time enough, as Gwendolyn grew older, to show her that between black and white there are many shades of gray.

I told Alan he had the analysis half right and half wrong. The part he had right was this: It's true that a very young child is likely to be confused if you tell her that some laws are bad while others are good. But it's wrong to conclude, as Alan did, that very young children should be allowed to believe that all laws are good. My own inclination is to go the opposite route, by teaching the very young that all laws are *bad*. As those children grow older and more sophisticated, they can be gradually introduced to the advanced Aquinean concept that some laws are actually just.

You walk a thin line with these things. I *do* want my daughter to know that policemen are good, in the sense that if you are lost they will help you find your way home. But I also want her to know that policemen are bad, in the sense that they enforce a lot of bad laws. I've talked to her about this paradox, and she has no trouble grasping it.

And there are some things that I want to impress on my daughter even when they push the limits of her young capacity for thought. The massacre at Waco took place only days after my daughter (then aged six) had asked me how the government uses our tax dollars. When she walked in on the television coverage of flames and carnage, I told her that now she was seeing the answer to her question. And when she heard that there were children in there, that they were burning children, her eyes grew wide with horror, and I both hope and believe that she will never forget that moment.

For those of us who like excuses to teach our children about history, Janet Reno and her thugs did the great favor of perpetrating their monstrous horror precisely on the anniversary of the Warsaw ghetto uprising. Cayley and I had a little talk that night about atrocities past, atrocities present, and atrocities future.

It is those emotional moments that impress themselves most indelibly on Cayley's memory, and it is *her* moments of spontaneous emotion that impress themselves most indelibly on mine. I read her a biography of Lincoln when she was five years old, and when I got to the part about his visiting New Orleans and seeing people in chains, sold like animals, she gasped in horror, and I was almost unable to go on, overcome by some emotion that was simultaneously transcendent love for my daughter and almost unbearable sorrow for all the sufferings of humanity. Years earlier, when I first read her the poem about "Wynken, Blynken, and Nod," I reached the climactic stanza where it is revealed that "Wynken and Blynken are two little eyes and Nod is a little head . . ." and her gasp of joy and recognition filled me with something equally inexpressible.

I wonder how many of our childhood emotions are first evoked by a poem or a story. Cayley been has moved to great heights and depths by the exploits of Addy, the "American Girl" of the deservedly popular storybooks, who escapes slavery to make a new life with her family in the North. Thanks in part to Addy, Cayley has a great hunger to know more about the Underground Railroad in particular, and about the human thirst for freedom in general.

Of course, she's still a child, and there are important gaps in her knowledge base. On her first day at public school, Cayley met a black child and came home to announce that she'd made friends with an escaped slave. We had a long talk about history that night, and we cleared up some pretty substantial misconceptions. I'm sure we'll have many more of those talks, filling in some of the gaps in the elementary school curriculum. I'm looking forward to them.

5

What Life Has to Offer

I LOVE READING POETRY TO MY daughter, and for many years—starting before she could speak and continuing until her academic and social calendars became full enough to compete with me for her attention—I would read to her almost every night, often for forty-five minutes at a time. We still do it as often as we can squeeze it into her schedule—maybe once or twice a week. Not only is she the only living creature who will sit still for my readings, but she actively enjoys them, and looks forward to them. I've always read her the poetry that *I* like, without censoring for content. We've read and reread Eliot and Yeats, and Gerard Manley Hopkins and Dylan Thomas. *The Waste Land* was her earliest lullaby.

Whether it was *Old King Cole* or *The Emperor of Ice Cream,* Cayley loved the sound of poetry long before she could discern its meaning, and I believe she will have memories like those of Dylan Thomas, to whom "the words, 'Ride a cock-horse to Banbury Cross,' were then as haunting to me, who did not know then what a cock-horse was nor cared a damn where Banbury Cross might be, as, much later, were such lines as John Donne's, 'Go and catch a falling star, Get with child a mandrake root,' which also I could not understand when I first read them."

There's more:

> What the words stood for, symbolized, or meant, was of very secondary importance. What mattered was the *sound* of them as I heard them for the first time on the lips of the remote and incomprehensible grown-ups who seemed, for some reason, to be living in my world. And these words were, to me, as the notes of bells, the sounds of musical instruments, the noises of wind, sea, and rain, the rattle of milkcarts, the clopping of hooves on cobbles, the fingering of branches on a window pane, might be to someone, deaf from birth, who has miraculously found his hearing. I did not care what the words said, overmuch, nor what happened to Jack and Jill and the Mother Goose rest of them; I cared for the shapes of sound that their names, and the words describing their actions, made in my ears; I cared for the colours the words cast on my eyes.

That, I think, was Cayley's experience—at least for the first few years. Then one night I read her Archibald MacLeish's *Ars Poetica,* which ends with the line "A poem should not mean, but be," whereupon six-year-old Cayley bolted upright in bed and demanded, "Be *what?*" She had discovered meaning, and her world had grown.

There are some poems that must have private special meanings to Cayley; she smiles serenely and knowingly whenever we read in Robert Frost's *Fire and Ice* of the prospect that the world will end through a surfeit of desire or hate. She knows that Thomas's *Fern Hill* is about the loss of a beloved childhood home, and perhaps she senses too that it is about the loss of childhood itself, though perhaps not, because although she finds the poem sad and beautiful, she—unlike her father—can hear the entire thing without being brought to actual tears.

Surely when she is lying in bed and hears the opening lines of Thomas's *In Country Sleep* she knows that a father is reassuring his daughter at bedtime in circumstances very like our own:

Never and never, my girl riding far and near
In the land of the hearthstone tales, and spelled asleep
Fear or believe that the wolf in a sheepwhite hood
Loping and bleating roughly and blithely shall leap,
My dear, my dear,
Out of a lair in the flocked leaves in the dew dipped year
To eat your heart in the house in the rosy wood.

Though with this poem, too, I'm unsure how much she grasps of the deeper and more tragic overtones—in this case intimations of greater perils which even a father is powerless to hold at bay.

I do think that she understands both the tragedy and the economics in Hopkins's lines:

How to keep—is there any any, is there none such, nowhere known some, bow or brooch or braid or brace, lace, latch or catch or key to keep
Back beauty, keep it beauty, beauty, beauty from vanishing away?

Reading Hopkins aloud, incidentally, is one of the greatest joys life has to offer.

I read Cayley poetry because it is an art that I happen to appreciate and can therefore communicate to her. I talk to her about mathematics for the same reason, and I hope that one day our conversations will inspire her to look on Beauty Bare in the form of the spectacular array of twenty-seven lines on a cubic surface that so fascinated the nineteenth century mathematician for whom she is named.

But there are limits to what I can teach her. My ear for music is extremely limited, so Cayley will need other tour guides through that territory. (We do manage to share an enthusiasm for the Grateful Dead, but her taste for Ace of Base and mine for Sondheim are probably forever at odds with each other.) What I do believe—and this is an observation grounded in economics—is that the most valuable thing I can do for my daughter is to give her a sense of life's possibilities, or (in the ugly jargon of my profession) of her opportunity set.

To that end, I grab every occasion to impress on her that each of her material comforts is the product of an act of genius, that cars and computers and supermarkets are all there only because somebody thought of them. I am trying subtly to create the impression that acts of genius are worth pursuing.

There seem to have been long stretches of history—most recently in the Middle Ages—when acts of genius were rare and economic conditions were stagnant. But then came the Industrial Revolution, in tandem with a culture of inventiveness that transformed the human condition. I hope my daughter will revel in the greatness of that culture, and choose to participate in it.

I want her to know that the strategy for success in life is to identify a need and invent a way to fill it. No artist or inventor or entrepreneur ever achieved greatness by performing an old task in the old way. This is a moral that runs at large through every level of endeavor: It applies to the assembly line worker who is constantly on the lookout for a way to increase production, as well as to the poets who blazed the trail of high modernism.

That lesson is not obvious to children; it needs to be taught. To an adolescent who got his summer job by filling out an application and having the good fortune to get selected from a large pool of essentially identical applicants, there is a temptation to overgeneralize and presume that the chairman of the General Motors Corporation got his job essentially the same way. It's a parent's job to combat that false impression and explain that corporate success, like success in general, comes to those who distinguish themselves from the crowd through the force of their creative vision.

That means that the executives of large corporations tend to be uniquely talented and irreplaceable, unlike, for example, the president of the United States. Corporate executives succeed on their singular ideas and abilities, whereas politicians succeed largely on their propensity to avoid giving offense.

Apparently, several Supreme Court justices were never educated about these matters. Their arrested development is displayed in their 1982 ruling (cited by President Clinton in his defense against Paula Jones) that immunizes the president of the United States against lawsuits for acts committed while in office, because those lawsuits would "hamper decision making" by the president. The same immunity does not, however, apply to the president of General Motors, despite the fact that he's a lot closer to being indispensable.

That's not to say that corporate executives should be immune to lawsuits; it's to say that *if* you were handing out immunity from lawsuits, you wouldn't want to put the U.S. president anywhere near the front of the line. In fact, it's hard to see how the time of a politician, who does nothing but shuffle other people's wealth around, could be more socially valuable than the time of *any* of the tens of millions of citizens who are actually doing something productive with their lives.

In a later (1997) ruling in the Paula Jones case, the Court ruled unanimously that the president is not immunized against lawsuits for acts committed *before* taking office. Even so, the Court failed to reject explicitly the ridiculous contention that the president's time is more valuable than that of a taxi driver, a professor of economics, or a corporate executive.

It's the rarity of their skills that allows executives to earn as much as they do; if their skills were common, competition would bid their wages down. To win large rewards, you have to make unique contributions.

I want my daughter to understand all that, and more generally to know that, by and large, the way she'll know when she's doing something socially useful is that people will be willing to pay her to do it. Social usefulness is not the only appropriate goal in life, but it's nice to have a way to recogize how you're doing in that dimension.

I once asked an expectant father what he hoped his child would be like, and he instantly answered "shortstop." Then he quickly assured me that in reality he had no specific ambitions for his child, beyond happiness and success in whatever direction life might take him—"as long as it's in the infield."

There was, of course, a twinkle in his eye.

I don't know what position Cayley will play in life, but I hope she'll play it with gusto. I'll consider it a troubling development if she brings home straight *A*'s from high school. An adolescent who's not neglecting her schoolwork is one who has failed to develop consuming passions, interests, and ambitions. Striving to craft a perfect poem, or to design a better bicycle, or to complete the New York marathon, is a higher calling than striving to pass a high school economics course.

Not to belittle economics. Economics is an interest that Cayley and I can share, especially when it's in the news. Cayley has long had a precocious interest in current events, which I am sure dates from the Gulf War, when she had just turned three and was acutely aware that all of the grown-ups who lived in her world had become strangely somber and attentive to the television. She wanted to know everything that was happening and to be reassured that it was all very far away. For many months afterward, she wanted to watch the news and know what all the stories were about. When she was five, I overheard her explaining to a twelve-year-old who Boris Yeltsin is.

Because many news stories concern economics, there's been a natural confluence of interests between Cayley and me. A lot of economic issues are easier to explain to children than adults, because adults carry with them a lifetime of prejudices. Cayley knows that the minimum wage law prohibits certain people from working; a lot of adults don't understand that that's the essence of the minimum wage. She knows too that the public television station is owned and operated by the government, and recognized all on her own that it is therefore likely to be a source of pro-government propaganda. By contrast, many adults seem to think it's just a coincidence that government-owned media tend to advocate expanded government programs.

Cayley understands too, as, incredibly, many adults do not, that the reason there are homeless people is that—for whatever reason—some people prefer not to acquire homes.[1] She scoffed when she heard a television commentator suggest that the problem is a "shortage" of housing; she's old enough to understand that when people offer to buy houses other people will offer to build them.

The night before Cayley started first grade, she had an attack of panic. As I was tucking her in, she suddenly choked back tears and blurted out, "I'm *scared* to go to first grade." So we turned the light on, and we talked, and I told her the story of a little boy who lived a long time ago. He, too, was scared to start first grade, and—well, it was a long story, but everything worked out well for him in the end. When I came to the punchline—that the little boy grew up to become her father—she was immensely comforted.

---

1. That is to say, either they prefer not to earn enough income to acquire a home or they prefer to spend their income in other ways.

The following year, Cayley enrolled in a Saturday morning gymnastics class that triggered a similar (but milder) panic attack. This time, I had no personal story to share. (Actually, if the truth be told, even the earlier story was pure fiction. I have absolutely no memory of what it was like to start first grade.) But Cayley is a devotee of economic reasoning, and we put her devotion to good use by analyzing the gym instructors' incentives: Unhappy children would leave the program, and the school would earn lower profits; surely, then, the instructors will strive to keep the children happy. That logic completely assuaged her fears. Fortunately she didn't stop to think about the fact that no such incentives would govern her new teacher at the public elementary school. The gym class, incidentally, was a great success.

We took a walk in the woods together years ago, Cayley aged four, and her dad, and her friend Jessica, also four. Jessica discovered a beautiful feather, and Cayley discovered envy. Well, surely she'd felt envy before, but she never had a name for it until we got back to the house, and Jessica left for home, and we found time for a father-daughter talk. Cayley—whose envy had been of the wistful, not the bitter, variety—knew already that when your friend finds a feather and you don't, it's better to be happy for your friend than sorry for yourself. But she was surprised when I told her this was a lesson many adults have yet to learn. She had never considered the possibility of taking Jessica's feather by force, and was accordingly shocked when I told her about the progressive income tax.

Little girls—and sometimes little boys, though I think not to the same degree—spend a lot of time worrying about who their friends are. Whenever three of them meet on the playground, one ends up feeling left out. Cayley's been through her share of those crises, and I've been through my share of vicarious heartache. If I can, I help her figure out what went wrong and how to repair the friendship. More often, all I can do is listen or wipe away a tear, or tell her the same thing I told her the last time: Sometimes two other kids want to play with each other and not with you, and sometimes all you can do is learn to deal with it; learn to cope. You can't force them to play with you, and even if you could it would be a bad idea.

That might work for grown-ups, she always tells me, but you don't understand how hard it is for kids. I have no real response for that—but I do note that someday she'll encounter a lot of grown-ups who are less mature than she gives them credit for. To every American manufacturer who seeks "protection" from foreign competition, I want to say that sometimes two people want to trade with each other and not with you, and sometimes the right thing to do is to learn to deal with it. Maybe you can force them to trade with you, but it's childish and wrong.

I'm always looking for new ways to teach economics to children, and to that end I have a proposal to reform the tax system. Here's my idea: You'll calculate your taxes just as you do today, but instead of writing a check to the IRS, you'll write a check to Toys R Us, in exchange for the equivalent value in toys. You'll bring the toys home and give them to your children; then after one week an IRS agent will arrive at your door, confiscate the toys, and return them for cash. I can think of no better way to educate children about what taxes are.

But in the absence of such high drama, a child can get quite an education just by extracting lessons from life's routine events—the first day of school; a walk in the woods; a playground tiff. Or a ride in the car: I remember Cayley, aged nine, primping in the vanity mirror and aroused to curiosity by my innocent query: How can light from her face reach the mirror if we're traveling forward? That was easy: The light must be going faster than the car is. But what if the car were going faster than light? Then the mirror wouldn't work! And then some discussion about how everything else seems to work equally well at high speeds as at a standstill—why should mirrors be special? And then, miracle of miracles, Cayley's own resolution of the quandary with the conjecture that perhaps cars cannot, even in principle, travel faster than light.

Sometimes she dazzles me.

Hunger and fatigue had caught up with me one night, and my complaints led Cayley to ask whether I was more hungry or more tired. My initial reaction was to explain that the question made no sense, because hunger and fatigue are measured in entirely different, and incomparable, units. There is no common scale for weighing them against each other. I know what it means to be hungrier than I was an hour ago, but I'm not sure I know what it means to be hungrier than I am tired.

But then I paused to reflect that in fact adults ask each other questions like this all the time, and other adults answer them, and both parties seem confident that some significant information has been conveyed by the answers. So we must have some innate instinct for converting our fundamental needs to a single one-dimensional scale. My crabbed economist's way of measuring human wants must have been inadequate, and I thank Cayley for making me realize that.

After I'd had a little food and a little rest, I reflected on the irony of Cayley's question. Unthoughtful adults have been known to insist that you can't put a dollar value on love, or on the environment, or on human life—which is just another way of saying that it is simply impossible to weigh such diverse concerns on a single scale. Cayley could teach those adults a thing or two. Deciding whether you'd rather preserve a rare species of monkey or have an extra $50 in your bank account is easy compared to deciding whether you're more hungry or more tired. And even a child can do that.

After an hour of uproarious roughhousing and laughter, Cayley and I were sprawled out on the floor, gasping for breath. I turned and asked her for a promise: Never marry anybody you can't have that much fun with. She agreed. Then I tickled her belly and we were at it again.

Let's see what other fatherly advice I can come up with.

I teach a freshman honors seminar that's in high demand. To get in, you have to submit an application with an essay. This year, one applicant's essay explained that he is a very careful and patient listener—because he has discovered that treating your opponents with respect makes it easier to win them over to your side.

When my blood had finished boiling, I summarily rejected his application for the course, and regretted that there was no way I could revoke his admission to the university. Nobody who views argument as a competition belongs in college, or for that matter in polite society. One listens carefully to one's opponents not in order to win them over, but to see what one can learn from them. Here was a kid who had made it all the way through high school without discovering that it is *delightful* to be proved wrong in an argument, and thereby to be enriched.

I briefly considered admitting him to the course in hope that I could show him there's a better way to be. But on rereading his essay, I became convinced that he was demonstrating not naive ignorance but an irremediable character flaw.

My fatherly advice, then, is to be as different as possible from this student—and as different as possible from the tens of thousands of readers who made a best-seller out of that despicably titled book *How to Argue and Win Every Time.*

Debate is like roughhousing—the point is not to win but to savor the experience. All my fatherly advice involves savoring experience. It's all about living with gusto.

Cayley was under three when I took her to see Disney's *Beauty and the Beast.* Near the end, when it appears the Beast has died, her tears were silent but heartrending. There was genuine deep emotion there—an emotion to be savored. In that moment I flashed back to a literary passage I hadn't thought about for years, from Whittaker Chambers's *Letter to My Children:*

> And once, in place of a bedtime story, I was reading Shakespeare to John—at his own request, for I never forced such things on you. I came to that passage where Macbeth, having murdered Duncan, realizes what he has done to his own soul, and asks if all the water in the world can ever wash the

blood from his hand, or will it not rather *The multitudinous seas incarnadine?* At that line, John's whole body twitched. I gave great silent thanks to God. For I knew that if, as children, you could thus feel in your souls the reverence and awe for life and the world, which is the ultimate meaning of Beethoven and Shakespeare, as man and woman you could never be satisfied with less.

This was a man who knew what parenthood's about.

All my advice, as I said, is about savoring joy—the joys of laughter, of deep emotion, of intellectual understanding and of creative accomplishment. Whenever I'm reading to Cayley and we encounter a new idea, I pause to remind her that all ideas come from people. What I'm really trying to remind her is that many people have found it worth their while to pursue ideas.

In first grade, Cayley developed a concentrated interest in continental drift. I'm not sure where this interest came from, but she acquired a lot of books about it and liked to have them read to her. While reading one night, I paused to reinforce my standard point about the importance of individual ideas. "You know," I said, "When I was a kid, nobody knew about this stuff. People just figured it out fairly recently." This grabbed her interest. "*How* recently?" she wanted to know. "Well . . . quite recently." "Was it after I was born?" "Well, no, it was before you were born . . . but not very long before." "Was it before you and mom were married?" "Ummm . . . I think so . . . yes." "Was it when you were a teenager?" "I'm pretty sure it was after I was a teenager." Now she went into deep thought and finally asked a clarifying question. "It was after you were a teenager but before you were married?" "Yes," I said. "Well, then," she asked, "was it when you were having sex?"

I'm not sure what six-year-old Cayley thought sex was. I asked her what it meant and her voice dripped with disdain as she said "I can't *believe* you don't know what sex is," whereupon I let the matter drop. Whatever it is, she was convinced it fits into a window between teenagerhood and marriage. I hope that in a life filled with gusto, she figures out how to expand that window—in both directions.

I hope too that she finds beauty in the places where her father has found it and in places he has overlooked. I hope she seeks truth. I have confidence that she will.

6

Cultural Biases

According to the book I've just been reading, we are living in the true age of faith. We flip a switch and confidently expect light to flood the room, never stopping to wonder why or how. We fly through the air, cook in microwave ovens, and surf the Web, all with little understanding—and often with even less interest—in the technology that makes it all possible.

The same book says that our distant ancestors were, by contrast, masters of their reality. When your most advanced achievement is an arrowhead that you've crafted by sharpening a stone against a rock, there's not much danger that your technological reach will exceed your intellectual grasp.

All of which is worse than nonsense. Among people who are alive *today,* there is not one in a hundred who can give you a coherent account of what really happens when you strike a stone against a rock, or for that matter what holds a stone together in the first place. Just sitting down on a rock—or a chair—and expecting not to fall right through it is an enormous act of faith for anybody with less than complete command of the quantum mechanical principles that make chairs possible. Unless you believe that quantum mechanics was invented in ancient Africa and then forgotten, you must conclude that until the twentieth century, nobody had any idea how *anything* worked.

You might want to respond that there are multiple levels of understanding. It's true that a Neanderthal man—like the average contemporary *Homo sapiens*—was unable to give a full account of what holds things together at the subatomic level, but he still had a pretty firm grasp of how matter behaves on a more familiar scale, and his world revolved around that knowledge. You might want to insist on the striking contrast between that prehistoric worldliness and the modern mindset which takes overhead lighting for granted.

You could take that position, but it would be indefensible. Let me prove that to you by experiment. Take a twig. Break it in half. Now put the pieces back together. Now let go. Why isn't the twig back in one piece? All the parts are still there, just as they were before you came along. Now that you've put the pieces back together, it appears that all the parts are in the same relative positions they were in before you came along. They had no problem sticking together then. Why won't they stick together now? What held them together before and why has it stopped working?

Either you can answer those questions or you can't. If you can't, then your confidence in the basic properties of twigs is a pure act of faith. If you can, then you are probably also the sort of person who has a pretty good idea what makes your lights come on. In either case, twigs are neither more nor less mysterious than house current, and it requires neither more nor less faith to take one for granted than the other.

Every age is the age of faith; every life is a series of unexamined assumptions. The sum of our unexamined assumptions is roughly what we call our culture. An unwillingness to question those assumptions is called cultural bias. Progress takes place on those occasions when somebody notices that an assumption has been unexamined, and pauses to examine it.

The prejudice that electricity is somehow more mysterious or less understood than ordinary matter is a good example of a cultural bias. The author of that book I've been reading learned as a child to take certain things for granted, and now asserts a willful refusal to be curious about those things. That's a warning that we should be careful about exactly which things we want our children learning to take for granted.

There is cultural bias in the prejudice that robbing liquor stores is bad but the progressive income tax is good—or at least not as bad as robbing liquor stores. That prejudice might appear to be nothing more than a simple and consistent belief in the rule of law, but it goes deeper than that. Lobbying for a more progressive tax code is well within the American political tradition, whereas lobbying for legalized liquor store holdups would be widely considered thoroughly disreputable. Either kind of lobbying is an attempt to change the law through actions that are entirely "within the system." We respond to them so differently because we are bound by more than just loyalty to that system; we're bound also by cultural beliefs about exactly how the system can be legimitately revised.

Cultural beliefs are passed to the next generation through education. My daughter learns in school that one-on-one stealing is wrong, but she doesn't learn that confiscatory taxation is wrong. The lingering effect of that indoctrination is powerful; I am certain that Cayley will never vote to legalize direct theft, but I can't be certain that she will never vote to raise other people's taxes.[1]

Reforming the tax system is an ambitious and honorable undertaking; rendering the current system unthinkable would be even more ambitious and more honorable. Success in that endeavor would require a revolution in cultural beliefs, ultimately sustaining itself through the elementary school curriculum. That's what happened with slavery, which was abolished through the force of arms in the short run, but rendered unthinkable through the force of moral argument in the long run.

The battle against progressive taxation will never be won by timorous politicians who argue—no matter how correctly—that high marginal tax rates retard economic growth and limit opportunities for the poor and the middle class. It will be won, if at all, as the long-run battle against slavery was won—by men and women with the insight and

1. Though I hope not. As Cayley approaches adolescence, I stand by the bargain I said I would offer on the day she was born: I'll make no attempt to dictate her morals, provided I can have complete control over her politics.

the courage to declare in public that progressive taxation is *wrong.* If people can learn to feel squeamish about stealing from a liquor store, they can learn to feel squeamish about taxing "the rich."

Cultural bias is both the parent and the child of intellectual schizophrenia. Ordinarily, when two contradictory ideas attempt to occupy one mind, they clash until one of them gives way. But when the opposing forces are clad in the heavy armor of cultural bias, neither can be dislodged, and they both take up permanent residence, crowding out the indigenous population of independent thoughts that might otherwise have thrived.

It is therefore a matter of concern to me when my daughter is taught on Monday that it is a vice to "take the law into your own hands" and then on Tuesday that it is a virtue to pick up trash from the schoolyard. Isn't picking up trash an instance of taking the law into your own hands? We have laws against litter and proper authorities to enforce them. But at my daughter's school, fourth grade vigilantes usurp those authorities, arm themselves with litter bags, and summarily police the playground.

Of course, the vigilantes are a force for good, Monday's lesson notwithstanding. In fact, taking the law into your own hands is almost always admirable, provided the law in question is a good one. If there's a law you want enforced, why would you object to people gratuitously enforcing it for you?

I suppose that Monday's lesson is motivated by fear that there are bad kids who should not be given a license for free-lance law enforcement, lest they interpret it in a way that is too broad and too self-serving. But by and large, the bad kids will do what they want to do, with or without a license. I'm more concerned about the good kids, the ones who are more susceptible to moral suasion. I want those kids to know that bad laws should be undercut, that good laws should be upheld, and that their assistance in both endeavors will be appreciated.

More importantly, I want kids to know that repeating words you don't mean is a bad habit to get into. There is such a thing as intellectual consistency, and it is a thing worth striving for, and it cannot coexist with slogans that are designed to substitute for thought. So I think we should not be complacent when children are encouraged to believe that words don't have to mean what they say.

Cayley has been taught that all endangered species should be preserved, but she's also been taught that the AIDS virus should be eradicated. When Cayley's third grade teacher required her to write a report on the endangered species of her choice, I encouraged her to choose the AIDS virus. (I was unsuccessful.) The AIDS virus is probably only one of many species that are not yet as endangered as they ought to be. We want the virus eradicated because its continued existence imposes unacceptable costs on its victims. That's no different in principle from saying that the snowy owl should be eradicated because it imposes unacceptable costs on producers and consumers of lumber, or that the manatee should be eradicated because it imposes unacceptable costs on those who would develop the Amazon basin. Some such statements are true and others are false; distinguishing the true ones from the false ones typically requires a thorough and unbiased inquiry into specific circumstances. Blanket statements like "endangered species should be preserved" are both silly and useless. And, because they inculcate the habit of substituting bias for analysis, those statements are dangerous as well.

Cayley has been taught that it's both a virtue to work hard and a virtue to be thrifty—never mind that for most people the only possible justification for hard work is to make thrift unnecessary.

The classroom emphasis on hard work and thrift makes me wonder what teachers think life is about. A student who took their advice too seriously would be certain to make the mistake of dying with a lot of money in the bank.

Next year, Cayley will be admonished that adolescent sex is a bad thing, but she will also be trained in how to avoid its consequences by practicing "safe sex." She is also admonished that adolescent crime is a bad thing, but her school does not offer training in "safe crime." ("Of course, crime is a bad idea—but if you do choose to rob people, be sure to wear a mask, and never use unnecessary violence that might escalate a misdemeanor to a felony.") She will be offered no explanation for the discrepancy.

There must be some reason why schools teach safe sex but not safe crime. Perhaps they think that students are more likely to be sexually active than criminally active. Or perhaps they really believe—despite what they tell the students—that unlike crime, sex isn't always such a bad idea. If that's what they believe, I wish they'd be honest about it instead of trying to scare my daughter half to death.

Through education, Cayley has been enlarged. She contains multitudes. Among those multitudes are general rules of conduct which are never useful in specific applications. Adults too can be pretty complacent about holding beliefs that, if examined, would seem jarringly inconsistent—if not in the strict logical sense then at least in their flavor. According to my casual survey, 80% of parents believe they can strongly influence their children's values, even though they are sure their own parents had no influence on theirs.

Most people have instinctive sympathy for the man who says "I tried for months to get a job and nobody would hire me. Only in desperation did I turn to theft." The same people have only scorn for the man who says "I tried for months to get a date and nobody would go out with me. Only in desperation did I turn to rape." There must be a lesson to be learned from that juxtaposition of attitudes. I suspect the right lesson is that our sympathy for the thief is misguided. Alternative lessons are possible. But I am struck by the number of people who manage to hold both attitudes without feeling any compulsion to reconcile them.

I have frequently heard it said that those who oppose legalized abortion thereby become obligated to adopt and support unwanted children. I have never heard it said that those who oppose capital punishment thereby become obligated to house convicted murderers for the duration of their life sentences. Why is the double standard not only accepted, but so complacently accepted that it's not even remarked upon?

Politicians who supported, say, the Vietnam War but avoided military service are denounced for their hypocrisy. By that standard, we should brand as a hypocrite any politician who supports garbage collection but has never worked as a garbage collector, any politician who supports AIDS research but has never worked in a laboratory, and any politician who wants to increase productivity but has never started a business. But nobody would seriously take those positions. Why is military service exempted from the general rule?

From listening to the radio, I've figured out that our two biggest macroeconomic problems are: (1) People don't spend enough and (2) People don't save enough. Commentators seem to have no embarrassment about expressing both concerns in a single broadcast. I wonder how they expect people to spend more and save more at the same time.

I've read that we should subsidize colleges on the grounds that college graduates earn higher incomes than high school graduates, and higher incomes mean more tax revenue. Of course it's also true that employed people earn higher incomes than unemployed people, so I guess the same logic requires us to subsidize every business that has at least one employee. But the logic never seems to get carried that far.

When Bob Dole resigned from the U.S. Senate, he combined a clarion call for smaller government with a list of his proudest legislative accomplishments, *every one of which* had increased both the size and the scope of government. Either he was lying about his political philosophy, or he was lying about what made him proud, or the part of his brain that's supposed to screen out illogic had simply ceased to function. But his audience took no notice, inured as they were to the modern tradition that political discourse isn't even *supposed* to make sense.

From that moment on, Dole elevated his simultaneous endorsements of smaller and larger government to the twin centerpieces of his campaign, so much so that it is just amazing to me that nobody ever called him on it. In the debates, for example, it seems to me that any thoughtful moderator would have led with a question like this: "Senator Dole, you say that what differentiates you from your opponent is that he wants a larger government and you want a smaller one. At the same time, you say that your proudest achievements in the Senate include the Disabilities Act, the Clean Air Act, and the Civil Rights Act of 1991. Putting aside the question of whether this legislation was good or bad, there seems to be no question that it all increased the size of government. Are you proud of any achievements which *reduced* the size of government? If so, why don't you ever talk about them? And if not, how can you say that you have any philososphical differences with President Clinton on this issue?"

I've been waiting for a long time for someone to ask that question, actually. It should have been asked of President Bush four years earlier.

I've been walking in the woods with my daughter. She's stopped to smell a flower and I'm a few steps ahead, so I'm first to spot the water. "Cayley, come look!" My voice creates a disturbance in the atmosphere, and a wave travels outward to reach my daughter's ear. She comes running. We take turns picking up pebbles and flinging them into the pond. Each pebble creates a disturbance in the water, and a wave travels outward to reach the shoreline. Each ripple is followed by another, just slightly smaller, and then another, and another and another.

Anybody who has ever tossed a pebble in a pond has had occasion to wonder why the whole world doesn't sound like a Wagnerian opera. Where are all those multiple ripples that should bring the sound to your ear once, then again just slightly quieter, then again, then again, then again?

Never, even in my most reflective moods, had I asked that question, until it was asked of me—when I was almost thirty years old—by somebody who already knew the answer.[2] Now that I am over forty years old, the question has come to seem so natural, and my failure to ask it so inexplicable, that I feel like I must have spent my twenties in a stupor.

But simple curiosity is rarer than you think, among both children and adults. Cayley, who knows all about ripples and sound waves, has never asked me why she hears everything only once. It took a Hubble and an Einstein to wonder deeply why the night sky is dark and why the daytime sky is blue, and their extraordinary curiosity triggered great events in the history of science. And in my experience, all children (and many adults) take unquestioningly for granted one of the profoundest mysteries of the universe (or at least of the human mind): the astonishing asymmetry that allows us to remember the past but not the future.

I once met a family court judge who was near retirement. Reflecting on a long career of dealing with orphaned and abandoned children, he had concluded that adoption is almost always the wrong solution. Decades of experience had shown him that, compared to children raised by their natural parents, adopted children have more trouble

---

2. Now I know the answer too, but I'm not sure how to explain it without first offering a short course in differential equations. It's related to the fact that the atmosphere has an odd number of dimensions (three) and the surface of the pond has an even number (two). If we lived in an atmosphere with four or six or eight dimensions, we *would* hear "ripples" every time we heard a sound.

in school, more trouble with the law, more trouble forming relationships, and more trouble in their careers. I asked him whether it would not be more relevant to compare adopted children with orphaned and abandoned children who had *not* been adopted. He said he'd never considered that before, and would now need to rethink the lessons of a lifetime. Now one could argue—and in fact I'd endorse this argument—that this particular judge was just too stupid to be considered representative of his profession, and possibly of his species. But I carry the memory of this incident as a reminder of how readily people adopt ideas and then cling to them without ever having given them a moment of anything that might be recognized as thought.

(I have wondered this, though: If the judge's decisions had been affecting people he cared about instead of strangers, would he have thought more clearly in the first place?)

Speaking of judges, I once watched a PBS panel discussion on how patients should be selected for participation in experimental drug studies. The panelists, including Supreme Court Justice Antonin Scalia, came from all walks of life—and allegedly represented all points of view. Now it seems clear to me that there are basically two positions one can take on this issue: Either patients should be allowed to choose their own treatment (subject to such incentives as the experimenters devise), or somebody else should be allowed to choose their treatment for them. The minor disappointment was that every single panelist—including Scalia—took the second position. The major disappointment was that no panelist—including Scalia—seemed to recognize that the first position is possible. They all assumed that some administrator would be including and excluding patients from the studies; each argued strenuously that the administrator should adopt some set of standards or another; and *none of them showed the slightest recognition that they were all in agreement on the basic issue* of whether there is any role for an administrator at all.

Personally, if I were facing this problem I would start by setting appropriate prices. If too many patients want to try the new drug, start charging them to participate, or paying them not to. If not enough patients want to try the new drug, start paying for experimental subjects. If some patients are better suited for the experiments than others, set different prices for different kinds of patients. Now let the market do its job.

You might like that plan or you might not; I want to concentrate here not on its virtues but on the mindset that allowed Justice Scalia and his co-panelists to forget that it was possible. They assumed their conclusion—in this case that only a bureaucrat can allocate a resource—and then quibbled over details. All were slaves to the pernicious cultural bias that makes Americans assume that any *really* important social problem must of course be solved outside the marketplace. They never thought to question that bias. Their curiosity had failed them.

I want to give an extended example of how the refusal to question ingrained cultural assumptions leads to bad analysis of public policy. Let's talk about the minimum wage.

The standard conservative case against the minimum wage goes something like this: (1) The minimum wage causes unemployment among unskilled workers. (2) Therefore the minimum wage hurts precisely that population which it is designed to help. (3) Therefore the minimum wage is a bad thing. I want to examine that argument, piece by piece, with an eye out for cultural bias and unexamined assumptions.

First, I am confident that the minimum wage *does* cause substantial unemployment. I remain confident despite a series of 1994 studies by a group of Princeton economists which raised some doubt about the matter. Their most widely cited study examined New Jersey fast food restaurants before and after the minimum wage increases of 1990–91, and basically found no effect on employment.

Critics of that study have raised a number of objections. For example, the Princeton economists had taken at face value the data they gathered through telephone interviews with employers. Later, other researchers examined actual payroll records, and discovered important discrepancies between what employers say on the telephone and what their own records show.

On that score and others, the Princeton group has taken a lot of criticism, and has made some responses, and there have been responses to the responses. This is valuable activity, from which much will be learned, but it should not be allowed to obscure the larger point, which is this: Every standard textbook in economics offers a multitude of solid reasons to believe that the minimum wage is a job-killer, and no single handful of studies can possibly outweigh that well-established body of theory and evidence. That's not to say that further studies are pointless: It's possible in principle that someday there will be *enough* Princeton-like studies to force a reevaluation of this issue. But observing a single episode in New Jersey is no reason to throw out everything we know about the minimum wage, any more than observing a single helium-filled balloon would be a reason to throw out the entire theory of gravity.

The second point in the argument says that because the minimum wage kills jobs, it must be bad for workers. But that's a leap of logic. Don't forget these are *minimum wage* jobs we're talking about; losing a lousy job might not be a whole lot worse than keeping it. Meanwhile, lots of minimum wage workers *do* manage to stay employed, and are presumably grateful for the minimum wage.

The right thought-experiment is to put yourself in the shoes of one of those workers and ask whether you'd like to see a minimum wage hike. Suppose, for example, that a 10% hike would create a 10% chance you'll be thrown out of work. I think it's plausible you'd consider that a pretty good gamble. You win nine times out of ten, and when you lose, all you lose is a lousy job.

If minimum wage workers really understood the odds, they might or might not welcome a hike in the minimum wage. With a little effort, a competent graduate student in economics—armed with some data on what the odds really are, and extrapolating from what we know about people's willingness to gamble—might make a pretty convincing case one way or the other. But in any event, conservatives are (perhaps unwittingly) dishonest when they pretend it's obvious that the minimum wage "hurts those it is intended to help."

That undercuts the second step in the argument and makes it hard to go on to the third: the conclusion that the minimum wage is a bad thing. If we're going to reach that conclusion, we're going to have to get there through a completely different route.

It's not hard to find that route. Suppose you're a small entrepreneur with, say, ten full-time minimum wage workers. Then a fifty-cent increase in the minimum wage is going to cost you $10,000 a year. That's no different from a $10,000 tax increase, and you're not getting any new government services in return for it.

A minimum wage hike is equivalent to a huge tax increase on a small number of people (the entrepreneurs), with all the proceeds paid out as the equivalent of welfare to their employees. If a tax-and-spend program that arbitrary were spelled out explicitly, voters would recoil. When it is disguised as a minimum wage increase, it sails through even a Republican Congress.

Depending on market conditions, entrepreneurs might end up passing on some fraction of that tax increase to their customers through higher prices,[3] and it's even possible (though not very likely) for the fraction to exceed 100%, in which case the entrepreneurs are net *winners* from a minimum wage hike. (Exercise for economics students: Determine the exact conditions under which this unlikely scenario can occur!) But that doesn't make the tax any less arbitrary or onerous, it just means that a *different* small group of people—the customers—are paying part of this arbitrary and onerous tax.

In such observations, there is more than ample reason to oppose the minimum wage. But conservatives shy away

---

3. The entrepreneurs don't get to *choose* this fraction; they are bound by conditions beyond their control. If fast food customers can easily switch to frozen dinners, then fast food prices can't rise very much.

from these powerful arguments, preferring instead to pose as champions of the working class by embracing the dubious proposition that the minimum wage hurts workers. They do so in deference to a pernicious cultural bias according to which those who defend even the imagined interests of the worker are presumed to be more "compassionate" than those who defend the real and legitimate interests of the consumer and the entrepreneur.

I envision a principled and popular conservatism which stands as the champion of all the oppressed, including those who are singled out to bear the burdens of government. The avatars of that conservatism will recognize and proclaim the injustice of asking one small group of Americans to pick up the tab for an economy-wide program of income redistribution. They will insist, without apology, that if the government wants to mandate a handout to low-wage workers, it ought to acknowledge that intention explicitly and fund it with a broad-based and more equitable tax.

To successfully frame the issue in those terms, conservatives will need to effect a substantial but not unprecedented revolution in attitudes—something on the scale of the revolution that overthrew the nineteenth century notion that a public execution is a suitable occasion for a family picnic. The new revolution must target the twentieth century notion that the right to equal tax treatment is contingent on your occupation or your income or your social status, and vanishes on the day you decide to go into business for yourself.

Among the detritus of that hoped-for revolution will be all political rhetoric that appeals to the interests of the "average man," as if being average were a prerequisite for having legitimate interests, or as if we should care more about fair treatment for strangers who are average than for strangers who are not. Those sentiments are so deeply ingrained in our political culture that it's easy for us to overlook how ugly they are. In the brightest of futures, they'll be as unwelcome as a hangman at a picnic.

When Cayley started attending Sunday School at our local Reform synagogue, I noticed that one of the other classes had been assigned to write an essay beginning "To be more like God, I will [blank]." The best essays had been posted on a public bulletin board, and they all had beginnings like "To be more like God, I will recycle" or "To be more like God, I will be kind to animals."

Hoping that Cayley's class would receive the same assignment, I talked to her about what she might write. I suggested "To be more like God, I will slay the first-born of my enemies." She didn't like that, so we edited it for a while and finally came up with "To be more like God, I will attempt to achieve dominion over the entire universe." (This is a *very* Reform synagogue, by the way. The fifth graders' "Holocaust memorial art projects" are displayed on a corridor wall, above and below a banner that says "Nazis suck." I can't fault the sentiment.)

Intellectual complacency is the disease. Platitudes are the vectors. The habit of irreverence is the vaccine. I hope that a child who has been raised to laugh at God will find it natural to laugh at intellectuals, politicians, teachers, judges, journalists, and even economists whose cultural icons have displaced their ability to wonder.

Irreverence, of course, is not enough. To see through a false intellectual construct is only the first step toward replacing it with a new one. I want my daughter to know that expanding the limits of human knowledge is an honorable endeavor, that it is an endeavor to which she can surely contribute, and that the first step is to free one's mind of the biases that stand in the way of inquiry.

7

Fairness I: The Grandfather Fallacy

THERE IS NO DOUBT THAT FREE TRADE is good for *most* Americans, and no doubt that it is bad for *some* Americans. So the party line among economically literate liberals seems to go something like this: "The gains from free trade are too good to pass up, but at least the winners ought to share their good fortune with the losers."

Thus, following the passage of NAFTA, Michael Kinsley wrote in *The New Republic* that "when a $16-an-hour American loses his job to a $3-an-hour Mexican," fairness and political prudence dictate that he be compensated for his loss.

Maybe Kinsley is right regarding political prudence, but fairness seems to dictate just the opposite. Here we have an American who has devoted his life to charging the rest of us $16 for something we ought to have been able to buy for $3. What *fairness* dictates is that he and others who have benefited from protectionism should compensate the majority of their countrymen who have borne the burden.

Motivated by the passion for fairness that I share with Michael Kinsley, I have a policy recommendation to offer. I propose that every American who lost his job as a result of NAFTA and other free trade agreements, having been revealed as a social parasite, should have a portion of his assets confiscated by the U.S. Treasury. The proceeds can be used to fund a general tax cut.

Protectionism allows the $16-an-hour worker to exploit the consumer via an arrangement that is perfectly legal but entirely unfair. It is therefore odious in the same way that legalized slavery is odious, though of course not to the same extent. When slavery is abolished, what does fairness dictate? The logic of Kinsley's proposal would have us compensate the ex-slaveowners, while the logic of my counterproposal would have us compensate the ex-slaves.

The Kinsley view is not without precedent. When the Northern states abolished slavery in the late 1700s, it was generally assumed that in all fairness ex-slaves should compensate their former owners for the loss.

Seventy years and one Civil War later, there was never any serious prospect of compensation for the ex-slaveowners of the South. This was partly because they had just suffered a devastating military defeat and were in no position to press their claims effectively. But it was also because the moral sense of the nation had evolved, so that slavery was widely recognized as *wrong.* Nobody felt compelled to offer compensation for the loss of unfair and exploitative profits.[1]

Today our moral sense has evolved still further. In polite society, it is acceptable to argue that whites—even those whites whose ancestors in no way benefited from slavery—should transfer income to blacks whose ancestors suffered. But no reasonable person would suggest that modern blacks should transfer income to whites whose ancestors lost their slaves in 1863. If you *did* suggest this at a cocktail party, you'd never be invited back.

By contrast, another guest at that same party suffers no social stigma when he advocates publicly financed job retraining programs—programs that require long-suffering consumers, partially emancipated via GATT and NAFTA from protectionist bondage, to continue supporting the displaced workers who had been exploiting them.

The next time your cocktail party companion gives you an earful of compassion for displaced workers, try asking him whether there should have been job retraining programs for post-Civil War plantation owners, and whether newly freed slaves should have footed the bill. When he looks shocked, ask him why an $18,000-a-year cab driver, after a lifetime of paying inflated prices to support the incomes of manufacturing workers who make twice his salary, has any more obligation than an ex-slave.

The prejudices of the party guest reflect a thoughtless disdain for consumers that is sufficiently fashionable to unman

---

1. Early in his presidency, Lincoln favored compensated emancipation, but he was motivated by practical politics, not moral necessity. And even when he endorsed compensation, he did not propose that the slaves should foot the bill.

the vice president of the United States. In his great debate against Ross Perot, Al Gore defended NAFTA without ever daring to utter the vaguely disreputable word "consumer." Instead he fought on Perot's turf, arguing (implausibly) that free trade could benefit workers in the very industries Perot sought to protect. Listening to Gore, I envisioned a timid eighteenth century abolitionist, unwilling to defend his cause openly, gingerly opposing slavery on the ground that a system of free labor might be better for plantation owners. The high ground of consumers' sovereignty went entirely unoccupied in that debate, even though it was Gore's for the taking.

The Kinsley/Gore crowd needs reminding that the reason we have markets is to facilitate consumption. Production is only a means to that end, and producers exist only to serve consumers. In market situations, the producer's profit motive generally works to the consumer's advantage, and therefore ought to be encouraged. But when producers pursue their agendas outside the market system—as when they lobby for protection from foreign competition, or when they demand tribute as a condition of allowing trade to flourish—they serve no social purpose and should receive no reward.

Reassessment increased my property taxes by 40%. My neighbor escaped unscathed. This led me to make some ill-considered remarks on the unfairness of it all. "You're right," agreed my neighbor. "It *is* unfair. Apparently you've been underpaying your share for the past fifteen years. You ought to make amends with a big donation to the town treasury."

Setting aside the larger question of whether tax burdens should be related to property values in the first place, I had to agree with him. There is nothing intrinsically fair about the status quo, and nothing intrinsically *un*fair about change.

Call it the "Grandfather Fallacy": Rhetoric about fairness tends (quite mistakenly) to "grandfather in" special privileges like my low assessment—or a union worker's protection from foreign competition. Even when those privileges are unfair to begin with, they get treated like moral entitlements just because they've been around a long time. That's a recipe for inertia, because it means that any attempt to *correct* an ongoing source of unfairness ends up getting assailed as unfair in its own right. According to the Grandfather Fallacy, my assessment can never rise and the union worker's wages can never fall.

Issues of morality are always clearest on the playground. When a schoolyard bully is caught extorting his classmates' lunch money and ordered to reform, we don't worry that it is unfair to deprive him of his traditional income source. Nobody—not even the bully's own grandfather—would defend that schoolyard version of the Grandfather Fallacy.

Nor would anybody argue that the bully was misled into believing he'd be allowed to rule the schoolyard forever; that he trained himself to be intimidating on that basis; that if he'd only known the rules were going to change, he'd have trained himself to be sociable instead; and that he is therefore exempt both from blame and from the obligation to compensate his victims. But take the bully out of the schoolyard, put him in a manufacturing plant, and, most importantly, give him the right to vote—and politicians will crawl out of the woodwork to smother him with grandfatherly love.

What I am advocating is a sort of "zero-based budgeting" in the rhetoric of fairness. Zero-based budgeting is the corporate management technique that requires each division to justify all of its expenses each year from scratch. The traditional alternative to zero-based budgeting is to presume that each department will have a budget pretty much like last year's. Like the Grandfather Fallacy, traditional budgeting treats the status quo as a natural starting point.

A zero-based approach to fairness means recognizing that a policy is made fair or unfair not by improving one man's prospects or diminishing another's; it is made fair or unfair by its conformity to some absolute moral standard. We may disagree about what that moral standard should be, but attempts to resolve our disagreement should be a lot more enlightening than "I have a right to my agricultural subsidy because it's been there for as long as I can remember."

Is it fair to reform the welfare system at the expense of its neediest beneficiaries? That's the wrong question. The concept of "fairness" properly applies not to a *change* in benefits, but to a *level* of benefits. The traditional approach invites us to ask whether welfare benefits should go up or down. The zero-based approach demands that we go directly to the question: What is the right level of welfare benefits? The answer to that question should be a *number,* not a word like "less" or "more."

"What is the right level of welfare benefits?" is a hard question. But to attack all cuts as immoral is to deny that the critical question could ever be worth asking. A reflexive opposition to all cuts amounts to nothing more than a defense of the status quo just because it *is* the status quo.

The great mistake is to say that because something is good we should have more of it. It might be that because something is good we should have a *lot* of it (unless of course it's very costly), but "a lot" is not always the same thing as "more." No matter how desirable your pet program, there can always be too much of a good thing.

So when somebody tells you that the government should spend more on welfare (or AIDS research, or student loans, or strategic missile defenses), there's one litmus test question that will determine whether he's fallen prey to the Grandfather Fallacy: Ask him how much the government currently *does* spend in that area. If he doesn't know the current level, how can he possibly know whether it's too low or too high?

On issues as diverse as rent control, unemployment benefits, and antitrust policy, zero-based reasoning is frequently absent, leaving an intellectual vacuum that the Grandfather Fallacy rushes in to fill. New York politicians talk about "phasing out" rent controls so that tenants can adjust gradually to the discipline of the marketplace. But if rent controls have been allowing tenants to prosper unfairly in the first place, then fairness can't be served by allowing the controls to linger. If fairness is the issue, then the system should be eradicated without apology or delay, and even then tenants should be grateful that we don't come after them for back rent; morally, they are in arrears for the difference between fair market values and what they've actually been paying. Gradually phasing out rent controls is like punishing a car thief by requiring him to drive his stolen vehicle a few miles less each day.

Advocates of gradual phase-outs might reply that they are motivated not by fairness but by pragmatism—a sense of what is politically possible. But it seems to me that these discussions of fairness versus pragmatism are invariably muddled by the Grandfather Fallacy. Take the issue of subsidized unemployment benefits. I'm tired of hearing people say that "fairness" mandates a high level of benefits, while "pragmatism" puts an upper limit on those benefits. The truth is more nearly the opposite: Pragmatism—that is, capitulation to political pressure—is why we have high benefits in the first place; benefits were raised repeatedly by George Bush, the champion capitulator of modern American politics. Complete elimination of the subsidies would be a compromise between pragmatism and fairness; pure fairness would go further and demand restitution from those who ate while their neighbors worked.

An extreme version of the Grandfather Fallacy has infected the field of antitrust law, where some corporate mergers have been prohibited because they might lead to higher prices (to the detriment of consumers) while others have been prohibited because they might lead to *lower* prices (to the detriment of competing producers). Taken in its entirety, the philosophy of antitrust law suggests that no price should ever be allowed to change; instead the market should be paralyzed by obeisance to the *status quo,* just because it is the *status quo.* That's the essence of the Grandfather Fallacy.

When it comes to tax policy, the Grandfather Fallacy can be particularly insidious. In 1990, congressional Democrats argued that fairness required a top marginal rate of 31%. They got that, and by 1993 they were telling us that fairness required a top marginal rate of 39.6%. What had changed in the interim? *True* fairness requires that we pin the progressive taxers down by asking them to tell us once for all what they would consider a fair tax schedule, and then not let them change their minds every three years.

The Republicans have been no more consistent. In 1990, Newt Gingrich told us that he preferred Reagan's tax code to Bush's and in 1993 he told us that he preferred Bush's to Clinton's. By 1995, when his party took over the Congress, Gingrich had apparently changed his mind, as he made no move to demand a rollback to the pre-Bush/Clinton tax schedule. The status quo has changed, but the absolute standard of right and wrong is presumably no different now than it was in 1990.

In fact, if the Bush and Clinton tax increases were as unfair as many Republicans once claimed to believe, they should be trying not only to repeal them, but to make the rollback retroactive to 1990. On the other side, if the Democrats really believe that the rich underpaid all through the 1980s, they should have made their tax hike retroactive to 1979.

I want everybody to commit to a vision of fairness in the tax code and to defend that vision consistently. In fact, I'll set a good example by going first: I believe that a tax is unfair if one man pays more than another for substantially similar government services. This means that the deceptively labeled "flat taxes," under which everybody pays an equal percentage of his income (as opposed to everybody paying an equal number of dollars, as the word "flat" seems to imply), are almost surely too progressive to be fair. I'd settle for a flat tax with a cap, so that nobody pays more than, say, five times the average tax bill.

If your notion of fairness is something else, that's fine. Tell me what it is. But don't fall prey to the Grandfather Fallacy by telling me that the tax code is *never* sufficiently progressive. Intellectual honesty requires a commitment to more consistency than that.

8

Fairness II: The Symmetry Principle

NOAM CHOMSKY SAYS THAT CHILDREN are born with the universal rules of grammar hard-wired into their brains. According to Chomsky, a child learns to speak by translating those universal rules into the rules of a specific language. That theory might be controversial among Chomsky's fellow linguists, but it makes good sense to me. I believe, for example, that every infant brain contains some universal version of the phrase "That's not fair!" just waiting to be translated into whatever language the parents can understand.

Children know unfairness when they see it, and can be relied upon to call it to your attention. Economists, by contrast, believe that fairness and unfairness are subtle and elusive concepts, hard to define and harder to recognize.

Thus we have a subfield of economics called "axiomatic bargaining theory," which is devoted to figuring out what fairness is. The research strategy goes something like this: First propose a precise formal definition of fairness (usually in the language of mathematics). Next concoct some highly stylized scenarios ("suppose that Jack has two apples and three oranges while Jill has *three* apples and *two* oranges . . ."), and figure out whether they are fair or unfair according to your formal definition. Then try to gauge how well those judgments jibe with the intuitive notions of fairness that we all grew up with. Now repeat with a *different* precise formal definition of fairness, and see if it does any better.

If they could penetrate the language, toddlers would feel right at home with axiomatic bargaining theory. That's because formal definitions of fairness almost always assign a central role to the principle of *symmetry*—the requirement that people in analogous situations should be treated analogously. It's that symmetry principle that makes children cry foul when somebody else gets a bigger piece of cake.

Children and economists share an intense fascination with fairness that would be unbecoming in a normal adult. Fascination breeds philosophy—the naive philosophy of childhood and the sophisticated philosophy of the economics journals. What's striking is that the naive child and the sophisticated economist manage to agree on the fundamental observation that fairness is primarily about symmetry.

As we develop from children into adults—I'm thinking here of ordinary, noneconomist adults—our attitudes toward fairness evolve in at least two ways. First, we discover that fairness is not the only thing that matters. It's unfair that sick children have to stay home and miss the baseball game—but it's nevertheless a good idea to keep them home.

By the time we're grown, we understand perfectly well that fairness must often give way to efficiency or expedience. The child measures the cake and cries "that's not fair!"; the parent, with equanimity, asks "What makes you think I'm *trying* to be fair?"

The recognition that there's more to life than fairness is surely a sign of healthy maturity. But along with that maturity there often comes another, more insidious, evolution in how we think about fairness: It's easy to lose sight of the crucial symmetry principle.

Let me illustrate with one of those stylized examples economists love so much. Mary owns a vacant apartment; Joe is looking for a place to live. If Joe disapproves of Mary's race or religion or lifestyle, he is free to shop elsewhere. But if Mary disapproves of Joe's race or religion or certain aspects of his lifestyle, the law requires her to swallow her misgivings and rent the apartment to Joe.

Or: Bert wants to hire an office manager and Ernie wants to manage an office. The law allows Ernie to refuse any job for any reason. If he doesn't like Albanians, he doesn't have to work for one. Bert is held to a higher standard: If he lets it be known that no Albanians need apply, he'd better have a damned good lawyer.

These asymmetries grate against the most fundamental requirement of fairness—that people should be treated equally, in the sense that their rights and responsibilities should not change because of irrelevant external circumstances. Mary and Joe—or Bert and Ernie—are looking to enter two sides of one business relationship. Why should they have asymmetric duties under the antidiscrimination laws?

When the law is so glaringly asymmetric, one has to suspect that the legislature's true agenda is not to *combat* discrimination on the basis of race, but to *foster* discrimination on the basis of social status. By holding employers and landlords to a higher standard than employees and tenants, the lawmakers reveal their underlying animus toward employers and landlords.

We've heard a lot—and I suspect more than enough (in the sense that nobody any longer has anything new to say on this subject)—about *reverse* discrimination, where the law distinguishes unfairly between blacks and whites. But we've heard far too little about *sideways* discrimination, where the law distinguishes unfairly between, say, landlords and tenants.

Here's why I call this phenomenon "sideways discrimination." Landlords, like tenants, come in all colors. Every box in this diagram is occupied:

Black landlords	Black tenants
White landlords	White tenants

Reverse discrimination means that your rights depend on your race (that is, on whether you're in the top row or the bottom). Sideways discrimination means that your rights depend on your social status (that is, on whether you're in the left column or the right).

There are two good reasons to be concerned about sideways discrimination. One is principled: Asymmetric burdens are unfair. The second is practical: A system that restricts your neighbors' freedom today can expand to restrict your own freedom tomorrow. Today, the authorities tell Mary how to choose her tenants; tomorrow they could tell Joe how to choose an apartment. Today they tell Bert how to choose an office manager; tomorrow they could tell Ernie how to choose a job. If Ernie rejects a job offer from a black employer, he'll have to prove that his decision was not based on race.

And why stop there? If the principles of affirmative action are applied consistently, they will eventually govern every aspect of the housing market, the job market, and for that matter the marriage market. In that surreal future, it will be illegal to consider ethnicity in your choice of lovers. Justice Department statisticians will scrutinize your dating patterns to make sure you're sampling a reasonable cross-section of the community. When you finally settle down, you'll have to prove that the spouse you chose is objectively more qualified than any other applicant. Once the system is in place, it can be expanded to cover gender as well as ethnicity: Mary will be hauled into court for marrying a man when a more experienced woman was available.

If that vision sounds implausible, remember that affirmative action in its present form would have seemed equally implausible not so many years ago. If it sounds like a nightmare, remember that it's already a nightmare come true for Mary and Bert.

I want to reflect for a moment on *why* the extended nightmare vision seems both so implausible and so grotesque. Probably it seems implausible because we anticipate that tenants (or employees or lovers), if forced to live up to the same standards as landlords, would rebel at the ballot box. Sideways discrimination thrives most successfully when it's directed at a small minority—like landlords. In other words, most of us don't stop to think about sideways discrimination because we figure it's someone else's problem.

The world has been down similar paths before. Pastor Martin Niemoller, after eight and a half years in a Nazi concentration camp, wrote these words:

> They came first for the Communists, but I did not speak up because I was not a Communist. Then they came for the Jews, but I did not speak up because I was not a Jew. Then they came for the trade unionists, but I did not speak up because I was not a trade unionist. Then they came for the Catholics, but I did not speak up because I was a Protestant. Then they came for me, and by then there was nobody left to speak up.

Mary the landlord might well thank God every day for the gracious good fortune that spared her from the horrors of living in Pastor Niemoller's time and place. But she has this much in common with those the pastor spoke of: Her countrymen are largely oblivious or indifferent to the fact that her freedom has been abridged. The average Joe gives little thought to the fact that Mary is denied the rights he takes for granted. Maybe that's because Joe is not a landlord.

Why do we recoil from imposing the burdens of affirmative action on Joe and his fellow apartment hunters or Ernie and his fellow job seekers? I think it's because we recognize that Joe and Ernie have a *right* to live according to their values, and that we cannot respect that right without allowing them to exercise it in ways we don't like—even when they are motivated by intolerance or bigotry. But if Joe and Ernie have that right, then so does Mary. And if

Mary is deprived of her rights, then it's incumbent on Joe and Ernie to speak up for her.

Let me very blunt about this: Affirmative action has been called unfair to white male job applicants, unfair to business owners who are innocent but presumed guilty of discrimination, and unfair even to its own intended beneficiaries. All or any part of that might or might not be correct, but none of it has anything to do with the issue I'm trying to raise. I am arguing that affirmative action is unfair to bigots, and that even bigots have a right to be treated fairly.

You and I disapprove of bigotry. But the private virtue of *tolerance* and the public virtue of *pluralism* require us to countenance things we do not approve. Tolerance means accepting the fact that other people's values might be very different than your own. Pluralism means eschewing the use of political power as a means for "correcting" those values.

The idea of tolerating intolerance sounds suspiciously paradoxical, but so do a lot of other good ideas—like freedom of speech for advocates of censorship. In fact, freedom of speech has a lot in common with tolerance: Neither of them means a thing unless it applies equally to those we applaud and those who offend us most viscerally.

Tolerance is ennobling, which is why we should teach it to our children. Pluralism is insurance against tyranny, which is why we should demand it of our government. To speak up for even the most despised minorities is both morally right and politically prudent.

And lest you imagine that intolerance can be limited easily to minorities (like bigots) who are exceptionally unsavory, reread the quote from Pastor Niemoller, notice who the Nazis picked on first, and remember that it didn't stop there.

When lettuce is expensive at the grocery store, shoppers curse the grocer; but they don't curse their friends and neighbors who won't sell them lettuce at any price. Nor do we often find the grumblers offering to set up their own grocery stores and offer lower prices. The grocer is called upon to go an extra mile by those who haven't yet taken a first step.

Resenting the grocer, while giving a free pass to everyone else in the world who has failed to offer you cheap lettuce, is at least a relatively harmless kind of inconsistency. But the same morally confused instinct arises elsewhere, and it's not always so benign. Every six months or so you'll see news stories about amoral profiteers who charge $7 a gallon for water, or some other outrageous price for some other critical necessity, following a natural disaster that cuts some community off from its usual resources. The news anchors and politicians are always in high dudgeon about this stuff, but I never see *them* trucking in any water, at $7 a gallon or any other price. If the amoral profiteers have an obligation to sell water at less than $7 a gallon, why don't the news anchors?

Here's a more insidious example of the same fallacy. The *New York Times* recently ran an obituary for a man who was described as "a spokesman and lobbyist for civil liberties generally and gay civil rights in particular." Here the particular contradicts the general, because "gay civil rights" is a euphemism for *restricting* the civil liberties of those who, for whatever reasons, would prefer not to do business with gays.

Apparently the *Times* obituarist is in thrall to the Orwellian notion that anyone who refuses to rent you an apartment is violating *your* civil liberties. That can't be right. If there were such a thing as a moral duty to provide you with an apartment, then almost every one of your neighbors would be in violation of that duty—because almost none of your neighbors is willing to rent you an apartment.

Suppose Mary constructs an apartment building and then refuses to rent to you. She's still done you some small amount of good: By taking in tenants, she creates vacancies in other buildings and takes a little pressure off the housing market. Compare that to the amount of good *I'm* likely to do you. I have no plans to get involved in real estate. I won't rent to you any more than Mary will; I won't even acquire any property that I *could* rent to you. But according to the law (and the *New York Times*), Mary has done you some positive harm, while I'm entirely innocent. That's crazy.

How can Mary have a greater obligation to rent to you than I do? Moral responsibilities, when they exist, are universal: They apply to everyone or they apply to no one. A law which is not enforced symmetrically can have no basis in morality.

Along the same lines, suppose you're wheelchair-bound and therefore unable to reach the third story of your favorite shopping mall. Under the law, the mall owner can be required to install an elevator to accommodate you. But there can be no moral sense to such a law, because it requires the owner (a total stranger) to help you overcome your handicap, while allowing me (another total stranger) to ignore your plight completely. The mall owner and I are equally indifferent to your problems; why should he be singled out to bear the entire cost of solving those problems while I go on my merry way?

To put this another way, the mall owner, by building the mall, has caused you no particular harm. It's true that you can't get to the third floor, but it's also true that until he built the mall there was no third floor to get to. Building the mall doesn't hurt you, so how can building the mall create an obligation to help you? The elevator can't be viewed as the remedy for an injustice, because no injustice has been done.

You might want to counter-argue that the mall's appearance did make you worse off by creating a new attraction that your neighbors can enjoy and from which you are excluded. But that counter-argument is based on the position that you actively dislike having good things happen to other people unless you can share in them. That's a pretty crabbed view of what constitutes an improvement in the world—and taken to its logical extreme, it would require that you be compensated every time anybody does anything that benefits anyone.

A closely related example: Small business owners are required to hire the handicapped. If that's based on some moral obligation—if, in other words, there is a moral responsibility to hire the handicapped—then the rest of us should be required to start small businesses so that we can hire the handicapped too. Instead, the law creates a responsibility which is imposed on some people (in this case business owners) and not on others—which means that the law itself recognizes that this responsibility has no moral foundation. When the symmetry principle is broken, all moral content falls through the cracks.

The word "oppression" pops up a lot in political rhetoric. Like intolerance, oppression is closely related to unfairness. The usual context is something like, "We're more oppressed than those other guys, and that's unfair."

It would be useful to have a standard—preferably a quantitative one—for judging how seriously we should take those claims. Let me propose an admittedly imperfect measure: You are oppressed in proportion to your net tax bill—the number of dollars you pay minus the dollar value of the government services you receive.

That measure is imperfect because, for example, it ignores the depredations of oppressive regulatory agencies, or the requirement—imposed on a select few—to comply with the affirmative action laws. But it's a good rough approximation to the burdens imposed by one's fellow citizens—and what can oppression consist of if not those burdens?

Oppression is always the child of intolerance. We place enormous tax burdens on the rich, and then console ourselves that it's okay because the rich are different from you and me. Well, they *are* different—some through extraordinary industry and some through extraordinary good fortune. But to conclude from that difference that it's okay to take what's theirs—in a way we would never countenance among children in a schoolyard—requires a dehumanization that is the essence of intolerance.

Once, long ago, a U.S. president proposed a sweeping overhaul of the health care system, managed by new government agencies and financed through a progressive payroll tax. His political adversaries denounced the system on the grounds that it wouldn't work, that it would limit choices, and that the quality of health care would decline. All those things were true, but all of them were peripheral to the central moral issue, which was this: No one should be forced to pay for someone else's health care.

That no politician dared to speak that truth is testimony to how casual we've become about intolerance and oppression. Those who differ from the norm in ways that are unpalatable (like bigots) have a diminished set of rights; those who differ from the norm in ways that are innocuous (like landlords or employers or the wealthy) have an enhanced set of responsibilities.

But it is in the nature of rights and responsibilities that they must be distributed equally or they are deprived of their moral stature. Children have to be taught not to punish other children for being different. By the time they're adults, they should have learned that lesson.

9

The Perfect Tax

CHILDREN AND ECONOMISTS AGREE that fairness is about symmetry. Keeping that in mind, let me start with a fable.

Manny, Moe, and Jack live on ten wooded acres each. They all want to build cabins. Manny and Moe are equally accomplished woodsmen; Jack has never wielded an axe in his life, and will perish from lack of shelter unless he gets some help.

Are Manny and Moe obligated to help Jack build his cabin? Some say yes, and some say no, but I'm not going to take sides on that issue right now. Instead I want to focus on the symmetry issue: Based on what I've said so far, could Manny possibly be *more* obligated to help Jack than Moe is? Surely not. Manny and Moe are different in some ways (they have different names, for example), but they are not different in any way that is relevant to the question at hand.

Because they are identical in every relevant respect, their obligations to Jack should be identical.

Now let me give you one more bit of information. After surveying his acreage, Manny decides to clear five acres and build himself a magnificent fifteen-room house. Moe, who has recently reread *Walden,* decides that he can get by with a single one-room lean-to, leaving himself more time to commune with nature.

Given those developments, would you now say that Manny is more obligated to help Jack than Moe is? Once again, I think it would be hard to make that argument. Manny and Moe have different tastes in housing, but that difference seems to be of no greater moral import than the difference between their names. So the symmetry principle dictates that their obligations to Jack remain identical.[1]

But if Manny, Moe, and Jack live in the United States, then they are subject to a tax code that completely flouts the symmetry principle. Because Manny works harder and acquires more material wealth than Moe, Manny is required to contribute more than Moe to Jack's upkeep. (Of course we don't literally require Manny to go over to Jack's place and swing an axe, but we *do* require him to transfer some of his own earnings to Jack, which amounts to the same thing.)[2]

---

1. You might want to argue that Moe's lifestyle proves he has a particular aversion to hard work, so it would be cruel to make him work for Jack. But you could equally well argue that Manny's lifestyle proves he has a particular attachment to working on his own house, so it would be cruel to make *him* work for Jack. Those arguments cancel and leave Moe and Manny equally obligated.

2. Of course, in real life, Manny doesn't literally build his own house; he works at some other task and receives wages which he uses to buy a house.

The great irony is that the progressive tax system—the system that demands so much more of Manny than of Moe—is frequently characterized as a manifestation of basic fairness. It's actually a manifestation of exactly the opposite.

Nobody would even consider insulting a child's intelligence with a whopping non sequitur like "it's fair for Johnny to get the bigger piece of cake because he played in the sandbox while you played on the swings." Children understand that how you spent your day has no moral relevance to how you cut the cake. But Manny suffers the indignity of being told "it's fair for Moe to get the smaller tax bill because he picked wildflowers while you built a house."

Take his money if you must. But don't compound the injury by expecting him to swallow rhetorical gruel you wouldn't feed to a child.

When it comes to tax law, economists like to say that there is a trade-off between "equity" (in the sense of redistributing income) and "efficiency" (in the sense of preserving incentives for productive behavior). According to the conventional wisdom, a progressive income tax is equitable (because it places higher burdens on the wealthy) but inefficient (because it discourages work). By contrast, a pure head tax (of, say, $3,000 a year regardless of your income) is said to be perfectly efficient but perfectly inequitable.

But it is an act of violence against the English language to describe as "inequitable" a tax that charges everyone an equal amount. In the rhetoric of tax policy, the word "inequitable" almost never means "inequitable"; instead it means something like "less redistributionist than the speaker would prefer." (I suppose it would be rash to expect anything like linguistic precision in a political climate where politicians use the word "flat tax" to describe a tax which varies in proportion with income.)

I reject the equity/efficiency dichotomy, because I reject the notion that there is anything "equitable" about the usual approaches to income redistribution. There's nothing equitable about a system that imposes different obligations on essentially identical citizens.

We are all endowed with the same twenty-four hours each day. You can spend each of those hours either earning income or enjoying leisure. If you spend an hour earning income, the system presumes that it is "equitable" for you to share a portion of that income with your neighbors. If you spend that same hour enjoying leisure, the system imposes no obligation that you share the benefits with anyone.

If I spend an hour earning a dollar, I am required to sacrifice, say, one third of that dollar to the communal treasury. If you spend an hour at leisure, you are *not* required to sacrifice one third of that hour to the communal good, say by picking up trash along the road. That fundamental asymmetry is the very opposite of what we usually recognize as either equitable or fair.

When differences in income result exclusively from individual choices, it seems to me that a head tax is clearly equitable, in the true sense of the word. But while choices explain a lot about the income distribution, they don't explain the whole thing. The reason I earn less than Frank Sinatra is not that I choose to spend fewer hours singing. Instead, through no fault of my own, I was born without the ability to carry a tune.

Some of us have more talents than others. If you are smarter or stronger or more ambitious than your neighbor, does it follow that the tax system should require you to contribute to his upkeep?

I'm not sure of the answer, but let me share the best argument I know for answering "yes." Let's start with a metaphor to capture the idea that we come into this world with social obligations: Imagine that it were possible, before we were born and before we could predict our stations in life, to (voluntarily) insure each other against landing in the shallow end of the talent pool. Imagine, in other words, that we could write contracts along the lines of "if one of us is born smart and the other is born dumb, the smart one will give the dumb one half his income."[3]

There is a good philosophical case for enforcing those contracts in the real world, even though they're never actually written. Courts frequently enforce the contractual provisions that litigants *would* have written if only they'd thought of it, and economists generally applaud the courts for doing so. If we enforce the contracts that people *forgot* to write, why shouldn't we enforce the contracts that people were *unable* to write only because of the inconvenient fact that they hadn't been born yet?

But you can't enforce a contract unless you know what it says, so the problem is to figure out just what contracts our unborn selves would have written. It's not so hard to think about that problem quantitatively. We have pretty good data

3. I am using "smart" to mean "endowed with high earning power" and "dumb" to mean the opposite. If I could think of a better one-syllable word for "endowed with high earning power," I'd use that instead of "smart."

on the real-world distribution of talents, so we have a reasonable measure of how much risk we faced when God was handing out the brains. And we have pretty good data on real-world insurance purchases, so we have a reasonable measure of how much people are willing to sacrifice to avoid various levels of risk. Armed with those measures and the back of an envelope, my colleagues Hugo Hopenhayn and James Kahn have estimated that at the Council of the Unborn, we'd all agree that about 77% of us—those with the most talent—should completely support the remainder. In other words, we'd all agree that 23% of the population should be permanently unemployed and on welfare.[4]

That's an amazing number. If you buy the argument about enforcing contracts, it means that the real-world welfare state ought to be expanded dramatically. But it turns out that by throwing just one extra consideration into the pot, you can cook up a new number which is equally amazing but in the opposite direction.

Here's the extra consideration: According to Hopenhayn and Kahn, we'd agree not only to place 23% of the population on permanent welfare; we'd agree also to support them so generously that they'd be *happier* than the 77% who work. But the Hopenhayn-Kahn calculation fails to recognize that this would lead to malingering—smart people playing dumb so they could go on welfare too. The whole system would collapse.

---

4. As this is written, Hopenhayn and Kahn are working to incorporate their very rough estimates into a more sophisticated analysis. The results of that research project are not yet in. In 1996, James Mirrlees was awarded the Nobel prize for his pioneering work of a similar flavor.

In other words, the disincentive effects of this plan would be so great that eventually everyone would starve. That's not a problem if there is some central authority who can accurately measure talents and force smart people to live up to their implicit contracts by staying off the dole. But if people can hide their skills, the original contract must be rewritten to avert disaster.

So let us return to our life before birth, and renegotiate our contracts. Here's the trade-off: We still long for that big social safety net. But we recognize that supporting the safety net is a burden on the workers, and we don't want them deciding that they'd prefer to collapse under the weight. We have to shrink the system in order to save it. But shrink it by how much?

Again, it's not hard to make some rough estimates based on the trade-offs that we see people making in analogous real-world markets. It turns out that after accounting for disincentive effects, we'd want to support an unemployed population not of 23%, but of just six tenths of 1%—in other words, practically zero. And that's not all. Even those few who were permitted to remain on welfare would now receive much smaller benefits. In other words, we would agree to dismantle the welfare state almost entirely.

It's all a matter of costs and benefits. A safety net that protects the bottom 23% is worth its cost—if we can somehow prevent it from being abused. But if there's a predictable amount of abuse (in the form of people pretending to belong to that 23%), then the whole thing becomes so expensive that we'd prefer to discard it, retaining only enough to protect the bottom six tenths of 1% (and in fact, supporting even them only minimally).

Six tenths of 1% is as amazingly small as 23% is amazingly large. Can we hope to unite such extremes into a practical guide to policy?

Well, yes, subject to a few caveats. First, the whole project makes sense only if those fictitious prenatal contracts carry substantive moral weight. I'm not *entirely* certain I believe that, but it seems reasonable and I'm willing to entertain it for the sake of argument. Second, we have to accept the particular numbers from the back of Hopenhayn and Kahn's envelope. That's harder, because Hopenhayn and Kahn themselves have only just begun to think about these issues and I'm sure their numbers will change as their thinking grows more sophisticated. But these are the best numbers we have at the moment, and it's not implausible that the final numbers will look something like the present rough estimates. So let's proceed, with appropriate caution.

My plan is first to list some tentative criteria for a redistributive tax system, then to design the best possible system that satisfies them, and finally to think about whether the result is palatable.

Herewith the tentative criteria:

1. *Ideally, there should be substantial redistribution from the most able to the least.* I'll include this, at least provisionally, even though it violates every gut instinct I've got—except for the gut instinct that says a good argument should always trump your gut instincts. Hopenhayn and Kahn have made a good argument.

2. *However, if redistribution has substantial disincentive effects, then it should be drastically scaled back—almost to zero.* This

rests on the same foundation as criterion 1—according to the calculations, it's what we would all agree upon prior to our births.

3. *Therefore, it's important to avoid disincentive effects.* This follows pretty clearly from criteria 1 and 2. If redistribution is so valuable, and if we'd be willing to sacrifice redistribution to avoid disincentive effects, then disincentive effects must be a very bad thing.

4. *We should tax not* actual *earnings, but* potential *earnings.* In other words, we should tax not effort, but ability. This one is doubly imperative; both efficiency and fairness demand it.

Efficiency demands it because a tax on ability is the clearest path around those disincentive effects we're trying to avoid. Taxing work makes people work less, but taxing intelligence doesn't make people dumber. (It might make them try to *act* dumber but that's not exactly the same thing.) The more general point is that taxes cause inefficiency when they discourage economically productive activities; therefore it is most efficient to tax not activities but immutable traits. If your behavior can't affect your tax bill, then your tax bill won't affect your behavior.[5]

Providentially, fairness—or equity, or whatever you prefer to call it—reinforces the demands of efficiency. Remember Manny, Moe, and Jack? Because Jack is less skillful than Manny and Moe, I'm willing to entertain an argument that they should be required to help him build his cabin. But

---

5. It's a bit of an overstatement to say that efficiency requires us to tax ability (or potential earnings); in fact all that efficiency requires is that we *not* tax effort (or actual earnings). A flat per-person head tax would be perfectly efficient.

Manny and Moe come into this world with exactly the same skills, which makes it morally untenable to require more of one than the other. Manny *chooses* to earn more than Moe, just as Moe *chooses* to enjoy more leisure than Manny. To punish either of those choices would not only be inefficient; it would also be fundamentally unfair.[6]

5. *There should be some reasonable cap on individual tax liability.* My own gut preference is that nobody should ever be required to pay more than five times the average tax bill. But I'd accept anything along these general lines.

This fifth and final criterion proclaims the virtue of liberty, as the first four proclaim the virtues of fairness and efficiency. It embodies the principle that there is some limit to our social responsibilities. Whatever duties we may owe our fellow citizens, we should be able to fulfill those duties and then move on.

By tacking on this fifth criterion, I've partly undermined the spirit that underlies the first. The original idea was to enforce the prenatal contracts we'd have written if we'd been able. There is good reason to believe those contracts would include a tax on the kind of skills that lead to success in the marketplace. Because the potential for success is unlimited—every now and then a Bill Gates is born—it seems that individual taxes should be unlimited too.

But let's not forget that this entire exercise is predicated on the human instinct to insure against bad outcomes. Guided by that same instinct, I want to insure myself

6. I am certain that fairness forbids taxing Manny's decision to earn more. I don't know whether fairness requires taxing Manny and Moe's skills, but the Hopenhayn-Kahn argument suggests that it does.

against designing a tax system that is founded on error. The Hopenhayn-Kahn argument tells me to redistribute, and I will do so because I think they might be right. But I want to set some limits to that redistribution, because I also think they might be wrong.

If God wanted to implement a tax system based on these five criteria, He could do it with ease. God knows everyone's earning potential, and can assign everyone a tax bill accordingly. And God has the power to make everyone pay up.

To duplicate God's tax code on earth would require leaders with omniscience beyond what we can expect to find and omnipotence beyond what we can be expected to grant. As mortals, without the knowledge or the power to implement a direct tax on earning potential, the best we can do is *approximate* the ideal tax.

That means taxing traits that are good *predictors* of earning power. For example, whites (on average) earn more than blacks do. A direct tax on income might discourage work. But taxing *whiteness* would not discourage anything, while still redistributing income (on average) from the relatively rich to the relatively poor. A tax of "$10,000 per year if you're white and $5,000 per year if you're black" is a perfectly efficient (and highly progressive) tax.

The correlation between race and earning potential is highly imperfect, as Bill Cosby could attest. We can bring our system closer (though still not perfectly close) to perfection by taxing maleness, height, and beauty; all these traits are positively correlated with income.

(In the case of beauty, though, it's important to tax only *natural* beauty; otherwise we'd discourage expenditure on shampoo, cosmetics, and dentistry. In fact, if we enjoy having beautiful neighbors, we might want to *subsidize* beauty rather than tax it; you can't always pursue two goals—in this case income redistribution and an attractive population—simultaneously.)

A tax on traits is highly redistributive, provided the traits are sufficiently correlated with income. It is also perfectly efficient—provided the traits are immutable, so that nobody will be tempted to waste resources in attempts to avoid the tax. And in practice, a tax on traits has an upper limit: Once you've paid your "white tax," your "male tax," and your "tall tax," you're free to earn all the tax-free income you desire.

You might think that taxing traits is a radical and untried proposal. But I'm not so sure of that. The Social Security system, for example, already taxes maleness, insofar as women receive more benefits by virtue of their longer life expectancies. And affirmative action is something like a tax on whiteness. It's not *exactly* the same, because affirmative action is more than just a pure transfer of income from whites to blacks; it's also an encumbrance to efficient matching between jobs and job candidates. But even though it's not exactly the same, it's not entirely different either.

Here is the strongest argument I know in support of affirmative action: First, the sanctity of prenatal contracts dictates an attempt to transfer income from the rich to the poor. Second, if they are based on actual income, transfers have an unacceptably large disincentive effect on workers. Third, avoiding that disincentive effect is sufficient reason to retreat to an imperfect substitute: by transferring income from the white to the black, we can at least *approximate* transferring income from the rich to the poor. Fourth, a direct "whiteness tax" is politically infeasible, so we resort to the indirect "whiteness tax" of affirmative action. Fifth, we recognize that the indirect tax creates inefficiencies by putting some of the wrong people in the wrong jobs, but on balance we prefer those inefficiencies to any of the alternatives.

To me, that argument—constructed and endorsed by one of my colleagues over the lunch table—is unconvincing to the point of being pathetic. But rather than digress into a laundry list of my objections, I want to salute the *spirit* of the argument, which (except for its glib presumptions about political feasability) is an attempt to construct a concrete policy analysis on a foundation of moral first principles.

But affirmative action is a side issue; let's get back to income redistribution. Ideally we'd redistribute on the basis of traits like intelligence, but that won't work because it's too easy to fake a low I.Q. test score. So we retreat to redistribution on the basis of traits like race, sex, and height.

As a practical matter, that's about as fair as a redistributive tax can get. It's broadly consistent with the Hopenhayn-Kahn calculations, and it manages to avoid punishing effort or impeding other free choices. If the trait tax is unacceptable, then so is every income redistribution program ever devised.

But something's wrong. If this tax is so perfect, why does it seem at least vaguely distasteful—not only to me, but to just about everybody who's ever heard me describe it? I propose to take that question seriously. If we can figure out why the perfect tax makes us squeamish, it should give us some insight into our feelings about taxes in general. So let's set out to explore the imperfections of this "perfect tax."

But how can there be imperfections? This tax was *devised* to be both a model of efficiency and an equitable implementation of prebirth contracts. So by the usual twin standards of efficiency and equity, the trait tax appears unassailable.

The appearance, however, is deceiving. I will argue in the next chapter that the trait tax—and therefore any tax—is open to serious criticism in both dimensions. Let me give you a preview of that argument.

First, efficiency is a mixed blessing. When governments can tax efficiently, they are likely to tax excessively. If the power to tax is the power to destroy, then the power to tax efficiently is the power to destroy with dispatch.

That's an argument not just against the trait tax but against redistributive taxes in general. If inefficient taxes are too costly, and efficient taxes are politically unwise, then it might be that no acceptable tax can be devised.

Second, we haven't finished exploring the logic of equity. There's a lot more to be said about the moral status of those prebirth contracts, and much of it tends to poke holes in the fabric woven by Hopenhayn and Kahn. It remains to be seen whether the surviving tatters suffice to wrap up an argument.

10

The Perfect Tax, Deconstructed

GOVERNMENT EXPANSION IS LIMITED by the consent of the governed. That consent is given pretty freely these days. In 1776, American colonists took up arms against a government far less oppressive than the one that now spends 40% of our incomes; if King George III had proposed the Clinton health care plan, his English subjects would have joined the colonists.

Still, there is surely some level of oppression that would impel even today's docile populace to revolution. A completely efficient tax system—that is, a system (like a head tax system) that imposes no disincentive effects—would allow the government to approach that level.

The problem with an efficient tax system is that it provides no built-in brake on the government's avarice. A government that takes $10,000 from everybody this year could decide to take $20,000 or $30,000 next year; one day we might wake up to discover they've taken everything. That can't happen under an inefficient tax system. The income tax, for example, is gloriously inefficient. If the government raised the income tax rate to 100%, we'd all stop working and they'd get nothing. To convince us to earn an income worth taxing, the government is forced to let us keep a substantial fraction of what we earn.

A head tax allows the government to take your money. An income tax still allows the government to take your money, but forces it to deliver an additional blow at the same time: You lose both your money *and* the prospect of earning it back through hard work. The politicians' desire to cushion that second blow may be the reason they don't take even more. With a head tax, that reason is absent.

So just as the alleged inequity of head taxes is no vice, their vaunted efficiency is no clear virtue. The efficiency of a head tax allows us all to be exploited equally.

The same is true of any efficient tax, including a tax on traits like race and gender. That's a reason to be wary of such taxes. But it's also a reason to be wary of *any* program that seeks to redistribute income. Remember the Hopenhayn-Kahn calculation: We'd want a huge social safety net—big enough to catch 23% of the population—but *only* if it could be constructed efficiently. If we decide to sacrifice efficiency in order to limit the growth of government, then our unborn selves would prefer that we sacrifice the safety net as well.

Here, in a nutshell, is the paradox: An inefficient tax is too costly because it invites malingering; an efficient tax is too dangerous because it invites taxation.

If we reject both inefficient taxes and efficient taxes, then perhaps our only option is to have no taxes at all, at least for the purpose of redistribution. That's a suggestive argument but not a conclusive one. We might decide that the advantages of efficiency outweigh the risks, in which case we can go full speed ahead with a trait tax. Or we might cobble together a compromise: Maybe we could construct some variation of the trait tax that is imperfectly efficient (which would make us want to scale back the safety net), but not *so* imperfectly efficient that we'd want to eliminate the safety net altogether.

Unfortunately, an inefficient tax system is not by itself sufficient to prevent the rise of tyranny; ask anyone who's old enough to remember the Soviet Union.

No matter how we tinker with the trait tax—or with any tax—it will always require a tax collector. Tax collectors must be invested with authority, and authority is always and everywhere the enemy of freedom.

That's something we would worry about if we were designing a world to be born into. We might worry so much about it that we'd abandon our attempts to construct an effective welfare state.

When we write contracts in the real world, we expect them to be enforced by well-established institutions like the courts, the police, and the censure of the public. But if we were to write social contracts before *entering* the real world, we'd have to *create* the institutions to enforce them—everything from the Internal Revenue Service to the Department of Health and Human Services. And if we had realistic expectations about the tendency of such institutions to expand and agglomerate power, we might just decide that we'd rather not write those contracts in the first place.

Hopenhayn and Kahn have told us that we'd accept redistribution, but we'd reject a package that combines redistribution with inefficiency. What I'm suggesting here is that what we're actually offered is a somewhat different package, but an equally unattractive one: a package that combines redistribution with a lot of centralized authority. Given a choice, I'm not sure that's a package we'd want to open.

Rational fear of an overreaching government is a *practical* reason to be skeptical of redistributive taxes in general. Now let me offer you a *principled* reason to be skeptical of the United States tax code in particular.

If there's one thing an unborn soul would want to insure against, it's being born in the wrong country—Cuba or Albania or Mali instead of Canada or Luxembourg or the United Arab Emirates. The U.S. tax code does exactly nothing to provide that kind of insurance. All it does is shuffle money around among some of the luckiest people on earth—those who have had the great good fortune to be born in the United States of America.

Even the poorest Americans have wealth and opportunities that would dazzle the poorest Indonesian (or for that matter, the average Sudanese). So if social insurance is supposed to compensate the least fortunate, we should be sending welfare payments not to East Los Angeles but to East Timor. You might or might not believe that we come into this world with an implicit moral obligation to feed the poor, but it is both repulsive and ridiculous to imagine that the strength of that moral obligation could vary with the national origin of the recipient.

I do not ordinarily contribute to private charities that concentrate their good works in the United States, because their beneficiaries—just by virtue of being American—are usually affluent by the standards of the world at large. But my government compels me to donate a substantial portion of my income to those same relatively affluent Americans. That policy is not the fulfillment of any plausible implicit contract. According to the agreements we'd have signed before birth, the typical "impoverished" American should be sending welfare payments to Tajikstan, not collecting them from his countrymen.

As of this writing, Bill Gates has an estimated net worth of $24 billion. On the conservative assumption that he's earning a net return of 3% after taxes and inflation, that gives him an investment income of about $2 million a day. Unless he has a phenomenal bequest motive, or a plan to take it with him, Gates ought to be planning to spend most of that income (he'll still be able to leave all the principal to his heirs, which is a pretty generous bequest). Of course, there will be some days when he feels more extravagant than others, but on any day when he spends less than, say, a quarter of a million, he's probably made a big mistake.

It's difficult even to imagine what it would be like to have that kind of wealth. But it won't be as difficult for your grandchildren. If U.S. real per capita income manages to grow at even a moderately sluggish 1.5% per year, then in fewer than six hundred years the average American family will have an income of $2 million per day. (That's corrected for inflation.)

More remarkably, if the United States could achieve the growth rates that have been reported by South Korea in the past couple of decades, it would take only about one hundred years until average family income approaches $2 million per day. If the United States grows like Korea, your grandchildren's children can live like Bill Gates—unless they rise above mediocrity and live even better.

Achieving and maintaining a Korean growth rate in the near future seems unlikely, but growth rates between 1% and 2% have been typical both in the United States and around the world for the past two hundred years. If anything, growth appears to be accelerating, and there are good theoretical reasons why it should continue.[1] The best forecast, then, is that your descendants will have to wait more than a few generations, but not more than a few dozen, to achieve a Gates-like living standard.

So each time the Sierra Club impedes economic development to preserve some specimen of natural beauty, it is asking people who live like you and me to sacrifice for the enjoyment of future generations who will live like Bill Gates. The Sierra Club's agenda is to take from the relatively poor (us) and give to the relatively rich who will succeed us.

But according to the philosophy of income redistribution, it's those wealthy future generations who owe something to *us,* not the other way around. If an implicit social contract allows the tax collector to confiscate one third of Gates's income, then surely that same implicit

---

1. See Chapter 13 for more on this point.

social contract allows the lumberjacks of the Pacific Northwest to confiscate your grandchildren's view of the giant redwoods.[2]

That's another reason to be highly skeptical of income redistribution as it is practiced in the United States. Those who would transfer income *from* the high earners of today, while simultaneously transferring income *to* the high earners of tomorrow, are not applying a consistent standard. We're therefore entitled to question their sincerity.

The conservationists are not alone in their pathological concern for future generations; the same impulse has launched an epidemic of hysteria over federal deficits. Everywhere you turn, there are people whining that the national debt is forcing them to live well at their grandchildren's expense. I have news for them: *nobody* can force you to live well at your grandchildren's expense. If you think your lifestyle is too extravagant, all you have to do is spend less and bequeath the savings to your grandchildren.

The arithmetic works. If the government cuts your taxes by $1,000 and sticks your grandchildren with the bill—say $2,000 with accumulated interest—you don't have to spend the $1,000. You can put it in the bank, where it will grow to $2,000 by the time your grandchildren withdraw it to pay their taxes.[3]

While it makes no sense to worry that *you* are living well at your grandchildren's expense, you might legitimately

---

2. I am accepting for the sake of argument the Sierra Club's presumption that it can accurately foresee what our descendants will value. But it's worth mentioning that for all we know, those descendants might *prefer* to inherit the proceeds of economic development rather than to inherit the redwoods.

3. See Chapter 15 for an elaboration of this point.

worry that someone *else* is living well at your grandchildren's expense. Maybe your neighbor applies his $1,000 tax cut to buy a car made of steel that could otherwise have been a girder in a factory that might have employed your grandchildren. Economists disagree about how plausible that story is, but we all agree that if you're out to protect your grandchildren from the national debt, it's basically the only story you have to worry about.

If you *are* worried about that story, it means one of two things. Either (a) you believe that your neighbor has no *right* to live well at your grandchildren's expense; or (b) you believe that your neighbor has that right, but you'd prefer to prevent him from exercising it. In case (b), I assume you have sufficiently little interest in moral niceties that you wouldn't be reading a book like this one in the first place. That leaves case (a). But if you believe that your neighbor has no right to live well at the expense of your grandchildren, you must also believe that your neighbor has no right to live well at the expense of Bill Gates. In other words: Nobody who agonizes about the national debt can consistently support income redistribution among the living.

Here, then, is the bottom line. First, redistribution is unacceptably costly, in terms of both efficiency and the centralization of power. And it's not possible to ameliorate both those problems at once: A more efficient tax code makes it easier for the collectors to exploit us.

Second, nobody seems actually to believe the philosophical case for redistribution anyway. If we think we're fulfilling an insurance contract, why don't we recognize that most of the beneficiaries live outside the United States? If we have a consensus that wealth should flow from those with more to those with less, why is there a receptive audience for the fervor of conservationists and budget balancers?

Nevertheless, we do have a progressive income tax, and it has become progressively more progressive since the 1980s. If that's not based on a philosophically coherent belief in redistribution, then what is based on?

The most obvious answer is that it's strictly a "might makes right," "you've got it; we're taking it" kind of thing. (Hillary Clinton made infamous remarks to this effect early in her husband's administration.)

But that doesn't explain the preferences of the many voters near the *top* of the income distribution who support higher taxes on themselves and on others like them. What could *they* be thinking? The question I always want to ask those people is: If you really want to pay higher taxes, what's stopping you? The Treasury will be glad to accept your voluntary overpayments.

If you believe that you and others like you have a moral obligation to pay higher taxes, then you must believe that failing to pay those taxes is the moral equivalent of theft. In that case, it makes sense to fight for a steeper tax code. But meanwhile you can live up to your own share of the obligation. To do otherwise is to say that you're willing to stop stealing, but only if everybody else does. That position is logically defensible, but it's pretty unappealing.

It's unappealing precisely because it violates the symmetry principle. It treats *your* stealing as less important than everybody else's. That is, it defines everybody else's stealing as so bad that it's worth trying to stop, but it doesn't treat your own stealing as so bad that it's worth stopping. That's asymmetric, so that's unfair.

The same unappealing logic pops up elsewhere. There are people who solemnly maintain that insurance companies are morally bound to write policies without regard to various preexisting conditions; those same people think nothing of shopping around and buying insurance from the low-cost provider—never mind that the low-cost provider probably got to *be* the low-cost provider by efficiently excluding applicants with preexisting conditions.

Are we morally bound to pay a bit more for our insurance so that those in higher risk categories can be insured too? If you think the answer's yes, you have ample opportunities to do your share by choosing your provider appropriately. If you think the answer's yes and you still choose the low-cost provider, then you're saying, "yes, there's a moral obligation here—and I think everyone else should meet the cost of meeting that obligation—but I'd rather not meet it myself."

I want to distinguish between two schools of thought. The first school says that there is a *moral* obligation to impose liberal insurance standards. Presumably that obligation arises from the contracts we know we'd have signed if we'd met before the preexisting conditions were handed out. That's the school of thought I've just been criticizing.

The second school says that there is a *practical* reason to impose liberal insurance standards: Any one of us could someday want to buy insurance after being diagnosed with a potentially disqualifying condition; we're willing to pay higher premiums to insure ourselves against becoming uninsurable.

To see that the two schools are really different, consider what would happen if all preexisting conditions were visible from birth: The first school would continue to thrive, while the second school would die out. My criticisms apply only to those who subscribe—or say they subscribe—to the first school.

When it comes to tax policy, there is an analogous distinction. One school justifies redistribution on moral grounds; wealthy subscribers to that school have no really adequate answer to my question about why they don't voluntarily raise their own taxes. But another school justifies redistribution on purely practical grounds—something like "If we don't give to the poor, their neighborhoods will breed crime or pestilence." Subscribers to *that* school can answer my question with ease: "The poor—and the attendant social problems—will always be with us unless we redistribute income on a massive scale." So said the most eloquent economist (and the most eloquent socialist) who ever lived. Here are the words of George Bernard Shaw:

> Many rich women, though they ought to know better than anybody that a woman can no more help being born rich than being born poor, feel guilty and ashamed of their wealth, and plunge into almsgiving to relieve their sickly consciences. They often conceive Socialism as a charitable enterprise for the benefit of the poor. Nothing could be further from the truth . . . . At present we give the unemployed a dole to support them, not for love of them, but because if we left them to starve they would begin by breaking our windows and end by looting our shops and burning our houses.

So now the argument comes to this: It is "fair" that productive individuals are taxed to support the welfare system, because without welfare those same productive individuals would be more often victimized by theft.

But that logic leads places where I suspect its proponents would rather not go. Try this variant: It is "fair" that attractive people should be coerced into granting occasional sexual favors, because without such a system, those same attractive people would be more often victimized by rape. Does anybody want to make that argument? Those who don't might want to rethink the Shavian defense of welfare.

In fact, the same analogy tends to undermine not just the practical defenses of the welfare system, but the moral ones as well. If it is intrinsically fair to subsidize with cash those who are born without the skills to earn a decent income, is it also intrinsically fair to subsidize with sex those who are born without the skills to attract desirable partners?

The potential to attract mates is an accident of birth, no less so than the potential to earn income. I suspect that, given the opportunity, we'd insure ourselves against bad luck in *both* lotteries. While you were waiting in line for your appearance and personality assignments, you might happily have signed a contract requiring attractive people—whoever they turn out to be—to feign interest in their unattractive neighbors.

I think most of us would feel pretty squeamish about enforcing that contract in the real world. Yes, attractiveness is a matter of luck. Yes, that luck is distributed unequally. Yes, we'd all have preferred a more equal distribution if we'd been asked in advance. Yes, it is possible, through coercion, to improve life for the least fortunate at the expense of their more advantaged neighbors. But does anyone doubt that such coercion would be hideously wrong?

Maybe we can learn something by thinking about *why* it's wrong.

Along with the gift of life, we are endowed by nature with talents and with dignity. By "talents" I mean the skills and qualities that allow us to earn a living, attract friends and mates, make the most of our successes, and recover from our failures; they include intelligence, beauty, perseverance, and an eye for the main chance. Although talents are distributed unequally, we each have a sense that the ones we've been given are *ours.* They belong to us. Dignity is the pride of ownership.

Perhaps if we'd met in a world-before-the-world, we'd have agreed to share the bounty of our talents. It does not follow that you can remedy the accidents of birth by enforcing that agreement. Enforcement means taking some people's property and giving it to others. But you can't do that without collateral damage: To take a man's property, you must destroy his dignity.

That's exactly why we recoil from coerced sex, even in fulfillment of a contract that we think everybody might have signed. In the real world, our dignity depends on the knowledge that our bodies belong to us. That sense of ownership is shattered if we can be held to commitments that we never actually committed to. In the same way, our dignity depends on the knowledge that the fruits of our labors belong to us, as a natural consequence of the fact that we own the talents that make our labors fruitful. To shatter that knowledge is cruel, and at the deepest level, unfair.

It's all about symmetry. What we know is wrong in one context must be wrong in an analogous context. Both rape and theft offend our dignity because they violate the rights of ownership. If you balk at one, you must balk at the other. And in the end, redistribution is theft. That really is why we don't allow children to forcibly redistribute toys on the playground.

I want to close with one more argument, which I'm not sure is right, but which I think is more likely to be right than wrong. In any case, it is quite separate from the other arguments in this chapter.

The other day, a bright nineteen-year-old woman told me that she would happily die at twenty-one if she could have unlimited income in the intervening two years. I told her I didn't believe her, because if income were that important to her, she'd be out earning it instead of chatting idly with me. She said—and this chilled me to the bone—that she'd be doing just that if only she could, but unfortunately there are very few *opportunities* in the area where she lives.

Very few opportunities! So this young woman had surveyed the world around her and found it perfect just as it was. There were no needs to fill, no improvements to offer, no contributions to be made. If we were all as oblivious as my young woman friend, she and the rest of us would live in caves instead of houses.

There is a trait—I'm not sure I know a name for it, but *gumption* comes close—which combines enough sensitivity to know what needs doing, enough inventiveness to figure out how to do it, and enough single-minded perseverance to make it happen. It's this trait that's lacking in people who are waiting for the right opportunity to come along, and in people who are very concerned to make sure they understand their job descriptions.

Economic growth is caused by technological progress, and technological progress is caused by gumption. Nobody knows what the world would be like today if Albert Einstein, Thomas Edison, and Henry Ford had never lived. Perhaps others would have come along immediately and duplicated their accomplishments. But I suspect otherwise.

I suspect, in fact, that world-class gumption is very rare, because it appears that *all* world-class talents are very rare. Consider baseball. Comparing the major leagues to the minors, it's clear that the 1,000 best baseball players are far better than the second 1,000. In a country of 260 million people, the 1,000 or so major leaguers constitute just the top .0004%.

Now imagine identifying the top 1% of baseball players—that is, the best 2.6 million players in a country of 260 million—and excluding them from the professional sport. The effect on the quality of play would be catastrophic.

I suspect—though I do not know—that something very similar would happen if we could identify the top 1% of the population in terms of gumption, and exclude them from participation in economic activity. My guess is that if you'd done this starting in, say, the year 1000 A.D., we'd still be living in the Middle Ages.

If my guess is right, then people like my young woman friend owe almost all of their prosperity to a very small number of scientists, inventors, and entrepreneurs. And it seems to me that we ought to account for that debt when we calculate social obligations.

I think we'd be willing to pay a lot to have more gumption in the world. But generally we *charge* people for being born with gumption, by asking them to pay more taxes than everybody else. That, perhaps, is a violation of an implicit contract. If that's so, and if implicit contracts are the basis for redistributing income, then perhaps our progressive tax code redistributes in the wrong direction.

Here's what I want my daughter to know.

I want her to know that fairness isn't everything, but I want her also to know that it's very far from nothing.

I want her to know that there is value in thinking deeply, from first principles, about what makes the difference between right and wrong.

I want her to know that economists have useful ways of thinking about things. In 1953, an economist named John Harsanyi invented the metaphor of social obligations as the fulfillment of pre-birth contracts. In 1971, the influential philosopher John Rawls used those contracts—contracts signed behind the "veil of ignorance" that shields us from knowledge of the particular traits we'll be born with—as the cornerstone of his *Theory of Justice,* which has dominated the philosophical literature on justice since it appeared. But to my knowledege, nobody in a philosophy department has ever thought to perform a simple calculation aimed at estimating what those contracts would really demand of us. We needed economists to think of that idea.

I want her to know that scholarship and ideology are both honorable pursuits, and that they can often be pursued in tandem. But I want her to know that when there's a conflict, scholarship matters more. So even though I believe that income redistribution is an evil, and even though I believe I have adequately refuted the most simplistic interpretation of the Hopenhayn-Kahn calculation, I cannot deny that the calculation leaves a lingering doubt in my mind.

I want her to know that shocking analogies are a great weapon against false platitudes. I have in mind the analogies between sex and income that I used above. Here's another, though I'm not yet sure what to make of it: People who must resort to unattractive sources of income—manual laborers, for example—earn our sympathy. People who must resort to unattractive sources of companionship—the customers of prostitutes, for example—earn our contempt. Maybe that means we should rethink at least one of those attitudes.

I want her to value gumption, to strive for gumption, and to be grateful for the gumption of others.

Cayley, be good. Leave the world a better place, through your thoughts or your actions, or whatever your talents allow. And don't ever raise other people's taxes.

11

Responsibility: Who Ya Gonna Blame?

IN THE UNITED STATES, GOVERNMENTS have not always been a force for good. Japanese-Americans were interned during World War II. Unsuspecting citizens were subjected to surreptitious radiation testing in the 1950s. For decades, Jim Crow ruled the South.

With varying degrees of success, the legitimate victims of such episodes have demanded reparations from the government. Their rhetoric appeals to a fundamental principle of justice: When a wrong is committed, the perpetrator should be forced to compensate the victim.

That's a good principle, but it's irrelevant, because the perpetrators of these particular wrongs *can't* compensate the victims. The jailers of the 1940s and the radiation scientists of the 1950s are in many cases long departed; in any event they never had financial resources sufficient to cover the costs of their wrongdoing.

It is *not* a fundamental principle of justice that when a wrong is committed, an innocent third party should be forced to compensate the victim. Personally, I've never interned anyone, Japanese-American or not. I wouldn't even know *how* to perform a radiation experiment. But I—and other American taxpayers, most of them as innocent as I—are called upon to pick up the tab when "the government" tries to undo past damage.

It's easy to say that when the government does wrong, the government should pay, just as is easy to say *many* things that are nonsensical. But what's really going on here is that John harmed Mary, John disappeared, and now Mary wants Bob to compensate her.

You might argue that Bob should be responsible for the actions of his government, just as a pizza shop owner is responsible for the actions of his drivers. But that's a poor analogy. A pizza shop owner chooses his drivers and their routes. Bob does not choose his elected officials or their projects; they are thrust upon him by the votes of his neighbors.

Expropriating the fruits of someone else's labor can be lucrative, but it's usually hard on the conscience. That's why nineteenth century slaveholders adopted the ideology of racism—it helped to soothe their moral qualms. Twentieth century politicians employ a similar strategy when they justify progressive taxation by demonizing its highly taxed victims as economic predators.

The same force is at work when genuine victims of genuine wrongs seek redress not from the actual wrongdoers, but from deep-pocketed bystanders who must then be falsely portrayed as somehow responsible for crimes they did not commit.

Consider the racial set-asides (and affirmative action programs more generally) that are defended, in part, as fair compensation for the legacy of slavery. Unfortunately, the costs of these programs are borne largely by white ethnics whose ancestors arrived in the United States long after slavery had been abolished. Racial preferences are not a way to erase the lingering effects of slavery; they're simply a way to transfer those effects from one innocent party to another.

I recently said as much to a roomful of undergraduates at Duke University, one of whom made the thoughtful observation that the oppression of American blacks did not end with slavery. He argued that even an immigrant family arriving in the twentieth century could have benefited (at blacks' expense) from the next several decades of segregation and Jim Crow.

There are two responses to that line of argument. Let me mention one and then dwell on the other. First, the United States is geographically diverse, and it may be difficult to make the case that Italian immigrants on New York's Lower East Side were beneficiaries of racial oppression in Mississippi.

The second response is less obvious but more important. It is this: Jim Crow was (among other things) a barrier to trade between the races. And economists know that barriers to trade are generally detrimental to *both* populations. Whites who were discouraged from serving black customers, or patronizing black businesses, or hiring black workers, or working for black employers, were *victims* of Jim Crow, just as their black counterparts were.

To argue otherwise would be bad economics. It would also be racist. Jim Crow prevented blacks from dealing with whites, and it also prevented whites from dealing with blacks. Who would want to argue that being denied the right to trade with white people is a form of oppression, but being denied the right to trade with black people is no big deal?

It's true of course that the Jim Crow laws were enacted by a white electorate, so one might be tempted to conclude that they were generally beneficial to whites. But that logic would require a theory of democracy that is at odds with all experience. Sugar subsidies, tobacco subsidies, peanut subsidies, and mohair subsidies have all been enacted by the American electorate, and no sane person believes that any of these programs is generally beneficial to Americans. Instead, they benefit small special interest groups with the political clout to exploit almost everyone.

It's true also that Jim Crow was about a lot more than trade barriers; it was about indignities large and small, from segregated water fountains to separate and unequal public schools. There's therefore little question that it imposed a far greater burden on blacks than on whites. But that's a far cry from saying that whites were its *beneficiaries* and are therefore in debt for the privilege of living under the reign of Jim Crow.

Here we have a political controversy that would not be controversial at all if we applied the standards of the playground. There, if Johnny steals Mary's sand bucket, nobody would think of ordering the innocent Bobby to make it up to her.

Cayley started preschool before she was two. I used to watch her from behind two-way glass in the parents' observation booth. Once, after my attention had wandered, Cayley was suddenly down on the floor and crying. The teachers came over and asked her what happened, but she just continued to cry. They asked the other children in the vicinity and got no response until finally another girl said "fell down." The teachers asked Cayley "Did you fall down?" Between tears, she corrected them: "A little boy pushed my down." (She hadn't quite mastered pronouns yet.) The teachers began to scold Eric, the only boy nearby. At this, Cayley gathered her composure, interrupted the teacher, and firmly corrected her: "Not Eric. Owen."

In less than two years on earth, Cayley had already figured out that blame ought to be laid on the proper shoulders. The fact that Eric and Owen belonged to the same community didn't make Eric responsible for Owen's actions.

(Though it's not particularly relevant here, I'll relate the aftermath of the pushing incident. About a week later, I was reading her a book. There was a picture of a little boy. I asked her what she thought his name was. No response. "Is it Danny?" A weak, noncommittal "No." "Is it Eric?" Same response. "Is it Owen?" She turned bright red, grinned from ear to ear, exclaimed "Nooooooooo," and shook her head with great vigor. The next night at bedtime, after lights out and after her story, she slipped into sleep with her eyes closed, quietly murmuring "Owen . . . .")

When one child harms another, children who were somewhere else at the time are held blameless. When one adult harms another—at least when he does so in the name of a government—adult taxpayers who were somewhere else at the time are expected to share in the costs of rectifying the wrong.

Why the double standard? More importantly, can the double standard be justified? I think that the answer is a qualified "yes"—there is exactly one legitimate justification, which sometimes applies and sometimes doesn't. It's this: Because it can be easier to get away with oppressing minorities than with oppressing majorities, it's therefore useful to have rules that say the majority must eventually compensate the minority for each act of oppression. Such rules raise the odds that the majority will rise up in the oppressed minority's defense.

That wisdom underlies the "takings clause" in the Fifth Amendment to the Constitution, which says in effect that the government can't take your front lawn and turn it into a park without paying you for it. (The exact wording is "nor shall private property be taken for public use, without just compensation.")

Or more precisely—because governments never pay for anything—the government can't take your front land and turn it into a park without forcing a lot of other taxpayers to pay you for it. First appearances to the contrary, the takings clause does not enshrine any simple moral principle like "thou shalt not steal." Instead, it says "thou shalt not steal from *one* person when it's possible to steal from hundreds."

A literal interpretation of the takings clause would forbid most taxation, because most taxation—and certainly all taxation for the purpose of redistributing income—consists of taking private property without just compensation. But the traditional (and nonliteral) interpretation allows that kind of taking, while forbidding uncompensated expropriation from a single landowner. If the takings clause were meant to embody a fundamental principle of justice or morality, there would be no basis for such a distinction. But if instead the takings clause is meant as a *practical* means to control political avarice, it makes excellent sense. A dishonest politician who can steal from one voter will not hesitate to do so; a dishonest politician who is forced to steal either from the multitudes or not at all may be driven by prudence to choose the latter.

That same wisdom has led me to propose a constitutional amendment capping everyone's tax bill at (say) five times the average; thus if the average American pays $10,000 in taxes in the year 2000, then no American could be required to pay more than $50,000 in that year. That would force policymakers to spread the burden of any new government spending among many taxpayers, and so insure broad opposition to the growth of government.

The power of the government is limited by the consent of the governed. The threat of revolution—or at least mass dissatisfaction—is a potent force for good. We can harness that force through laws and institutions—like the takings clause or my tax-cap amendement—which require each new government burden to be widely shared. Politicians are less likely to risk annoying 60% of the electorate than 10%.

After-the-fact reparations for government wrongdoing can harness that same force for good. Voters who are taxed today to pay for the wrongs of yesterday will be more vigilant about opposing the wrongs of today, lest they be taxed to pay for them tomorrow. The playground analogy would be a rule that all children must be punished when any one of them misbehaves. (Such rules have been employed successfully in occupied war zones and prisoner-of-war camps.) That rule can be an effective way to get the kids to police each other's behavior, and might be defensible on those grounds. But it would be a lie to call it fair.

12

Bequests

METAPHORS, LIKE MAGIC TRICKS, MAY dazzle through deceit. Consider the recurring metaphor that likens society to an extended family (with, more often than not, the speaker or his cronies as heads of the household). According to the accompanying patter, families do not allow one member to prosper while another struggles; ergo we need something like a more extensive welfare system or a more progressive tax code.

Note the rhetorical sleight-of-hand. While you were still pondering whether society is really like a family, I slipped in the wholly invented "fact" that families take from the rich and give to the poor. The truth, at least as it is revealed by last wills and testaments, is otherwise. Apparently most parental estates are divided equally among the children, even when some children are much wealthier than others.[1] A bequest is a final opportunity to redistribute income among those you love the most; if most parents reject that opportunity, then it's pretty hard to see anything "familial" in using the tax system to redistribute income among strangers.

A conjurer might respond that bequests are unimportant compared with other gifts that parents give their children—gifts like time, attention, schooling, and even cash. Sometimes those gifts are parceled out quite unequally. So—the conjurer argues—the family might still function as a welfare state, even if bequests are not the preferred medium for making transfer payments.

But what then *is* the medium? Could it be schooling? Let's think about that. Who would you rather send to college: your smart kid, who can make the most of an education, or your dumb kid, who needs all the help he can get? The answer—even if you have an egalitarian impulse to pour resources into the dumb kid—is to send the smart kid to college and make it up to the dumb kid through bequests (or other cash gifts). That strategy maximizes total family income, which allows you to do more good for *both* your children. So even if parents really wanted to equalize their children's incomes, they wouldn't do it by sending the dumb kid to a better school.

---

1. The evidence on this is scantier than I would prefer. I am aware of roughly a half dozen studies of estate division, and most have found that, at least in families with substantial assets, equal division is the rule. One study found an exception among lower-income families in Ohio, where there were a substantial number of unequal divisions. I have wondered whether this is because families at the lower end of the income scale invest more effort in convincing themselves that justice calls for redistribution.

Okay, if not schooling, then what about time and attention? We have good reason to believe those gifts are valuable, because we suspect that children from small families get more of them, and we know that children from small families do better in school. My one child starts with a substantial advantage over my neighbor's two, and they in turn have an advantage over my other neighbor's three.

There's a myth that firstborn children are far more successful, on average, than their younger siblings. The truth is that children like my daughter, with no siblings at all, are by far the most successful. Because such children are frequently counted as "firstborns," they inflate the performance statistics and make firstborns look good. But if all those high-achieving children from one-child families were counted as lastborns, it's the lastborns who would look a lot better.

In large families, both firstborns and lastborns perform substantially better on reading and vocabulary tests than their middle siblings. Presumably this is because the firstborn and the lastborn each get to spend a few years as something like an only child.

The success of only children suggests that time and attention are valuable, and because they are valuable, parents might use them as a vehicle for redistribution—giving more time and attention to their less well endowed children. But there are a couple of reasons to suspect otherwise. First, there's a good chance that time and attention, like schooling, are most valuable when they are lavished on the most able children. Second, even if parents wanted to redirect their time and attention to the neediest children, they'd often have a tough time following through—because it's usually the firstborns and lastborns who reap windfall harvests of time and attention, regardless of whether they are particularly needy.

So the general rule is that the best way to redistribute income is not through schooling or attention; it's through bequests. If parents wanted to redistribute income, they'd use bequests as the vehicle. But it appears that very few parents use bequests to redistribute. I think we're entitled to conclude that parents don't consider redistributing income to be terribly important.

Several rounds of counterarguments and counter-counter arguments could be made here. I've argued that when people divide their estates equally, they are rejecting an opportunity to redistribute income. You could reasonably respond that on the contrary, equal division of estates amounts to an *acceptance* of income redistribution; if parents really disliked redistribution, they'd leave larger shares to their wealthier children in order to offset the ravages of the progressive tax system. But a complete analysis would also have to account for the fact that parents who care about the size of their total after-tax bequest would tend to leave more to children in low tax brackets, and the fact that they don't do so is further evidence that they prefer not to redistribute, even when they are rewarded by the tax code for redistribution.

In any event, the U.S. government redistributes income among strangers to a far greater extent than American parents redistribute among their own children. If the politicians want our society to be more like a family, their first step should be to make the tax system less progressive.

I've called it a general rule that if parents wanted to redistribute, they wouldn't use schooling and attention; they'd use bequests. There's one exception to that general rule: In relatively poor families, where bequests and cash gifts are necessarily insubstantial, schooling and attention might be the only media available for redistribution.

If that theory is correct, it has some surprising implications. For example, we should expect wealthy college students to be smarter than poor ones, even if wealthy children on average are no smarter than poor children on average. That's because whenever a wealthy family sends only one of two children to college, it sends the smart one (making it up to the dumb one in some other way); but when a poor family sends only one of two children to college, it sometimes sends the dumb one (to compensate him for being dumb).

Another implication is that programs like Head Start should be less effective than their designers expect. When little Johnny reaps a windfall by being accepted into the Head Start program, his parents compensate his brothers and sisters by spending more time with them at Johnny's expense.

Incidentally, there's a nice irony here. By and large, the folks who want to argue that most people are instinctively redistributionist are the same folks who want to argue for the efficacy of programs like Head Start. But the stronger the redistributionist instincts of Johnny's parents, the less he'll gain from the Head Start program.

If parents don't use bequests to equalize their children's incomes, what *do* they use them for? What logic leads parents to divide their estates as they do?

I like the theory that parents believe there is something intrinsically *fair* about giving equal amounts to everyone. But to test that theory, we'd need to know more about the distribution of parental gifts—including schooling, time, and attention—while the parents are still alive. I don't know whether my pet theory would survive that test.

An alternative theory is that a bequest is a mistake. According to this theory, parents would prefer to spend everything they've got before they go. The only reason there's anything left over is that death arrives unexpectedly. But if this alternative were correct, we'd see old people using all their savings to purchase annuities that pay them a guaranteed income for life. The limited market for such annuities suggests that people prefer to leave something behind.

Yet another theory is that parents are governed by a "strategic bequest motive," using their estates to purchase attention from their grown children. The threat of disinheritance keeps those children in line; when the threat is effective, nobody is actually disinherited. Here's one reason to believe this theory: Economists have found that parents with a lot of bequeathable wealth (stocks, bonds, etc.) get far more visits from their children than parents with an equal amount of nonbequeathable wealth (such as pensions). The strategic bequest motive does not unambiguously predict equal division of estates, but it doesn't preclude that outcome either.

Parallel to the strategic bequest motive, we can hypothesize a "strategic gift motive" that operates while the parents are still alive. Those children who are struggling, and hence more likely to burden their parents (say by returning to live with them) get extra help in hopes that the children will become self-sufficient. (As a variation on this theme, one can imagine a "strategic schooling motive," whereby the least accomplished children get extra schooling, in hopes that the children will become more interesting to converse with.) At bequest time, the strategic gift motive would evaporate and the favored child would be favored no longer.

Bequest motives interact with economic policy in surprising ways. The effects of a deficit-financed tax cut can depend on whether most parents are altruistic or strategic. Altruistic parents would save the money from their tax cuts and leave it to the children who must pay off all that government debt someday; that saving would hold interest rates down. Strategic parents might spend a large portion of their tax cuts, causing interest rates to rise.

It's that interaction with fiscal policy that has drawn economists' attention to bequest motives in recent years. But a deeper reason for investigating bequests is that they reveal something about people's instinctive sense of justice. That instinctive sense is the best guide we have to economic policy in every sphere.

13

People Wanted

TED BAXTER, THE ANCHORMAN ON THE old *Mary Tyler Moore* show, planned to have six children in hopes that one of them would grow up to solve the world's population problem. Ted was a poor newscaster but a natural economist. His basic insight was impeccable: People solve problems, and when there are more people, more problems get solved.

The reason you are wealthier than your grandparents, and the reason your grandchildren will be wealthier than you, is that each generation free rides on the inventiveness of its ancestors. A generation ago, your parents were free to choose among three television channels, probably broadcasting in black and white, showing programs that could not be taped for later viewing. They used electric typewriters, of which the latest models featured a marvelous innovaton: a "delete" key that enabled you to automatically erase the last character you had typed. If you wanted to erase the character *before* that one you were out of luck.

For a lot of the comforts we enjoy today, we can be grateful to the inventors of cable television, video recorders, and the personal computer—and to the stroke of good fortune that prevented their parents from joining Zero Population Growth.

The engine of prosperity is technological progress—not just feats of engineering but also the design of new insurance contracts, better legal systems, and improved patterns of crop rotation. And the engine of technological progress is people. Ideas come from people. The more people, the more ideas. The more ideas, the more we prosper.

Michael Kremer, an economist at MIT, has gathered data from a million years of human history to support the theory that population growth drives technological progress, technological progress drives economic growth, and—to complete the virtuous circle—economic growth drives population growth, because wealthier communities can support more children. Professor Kremer's research leads him to quote Ted Baxter with approval.

Professor Kremer bases his argument on the presumption that a world with twice as many people will have twice as many natural-born geniuses. Thus a bigger population develops better technology for the same reason that the biggest high schools usually have the best football teams. But it's even better than that. A great quarterback is a great quarterback, but a great inventor can teach *everyone* to be more productive. And the quarterback's contribution ends when he graduates, but the inventor's contribution lives on forever.

There are two reasons why the gains from population size could exceed even the optimistic estimates of Professor Kremer. First, geniuses tend to inspire each other, so that 2,000 geniuses might generate *more* than twice as many ideas as 1,000 could.[1] Second, a larger population means a larger market for inventions, and hence an incentive for inventors to work harder. So population growth not only adds to the number of natural born geniuses—it also encourages those of us with more ordinary talents to stretch those talents to their limits.

In fact, two economists at the Federal Reserve Bank of Richmond, in research recently published by the *American Economic Review,* argue that the Industrial Revolution—and the massive ongoing growth spurt that it triggered—had to wait until world markets grew big enough to reward large scale innovation by entrepreneurs.

Since the Industrial Revolution (roughly two hundred years ago) U.S. per capita income has grown at rates of between 1% and 2% a year after adjusting for inflation. As a result, real (that is, inflation-adjusted) U.S. per capita income is now over twenty times what it was in George Washington's day and six times what it was at the dawn of the twentieth century. Worldwide, per capita income has grown roughly tenfold in the past two hundred years.

To get a better idea of what those growth rates mean, consider a middle-class American earning $50,000 a year who expects his children, twenty-five years from now, to

---

1. On the other hand, one could argue that geniuses also tend to intimidate each other; why spend your youth working to develop cold fusion if the genius next door is likely to beat you to it and get the patent?

occupy the same middling rung on the economic ladder. With a modest 1.5% per capita growth rate, those children will earn the (inflation-adjusted) equivalent of $73,000 per year; their children in turn will earn the equivalent of $106,000.

If it seems implausible to you that we could generate that much wealth so quickly, keep in mind that it's an extrapolation of a two-hundred-year-old trend (in fact, the assumption of a 1.5% growth rate shades the extrapolation downward). Keep in mind too that every historical advance has seemed implausible until it happened. In the first century A.D., Julius Frontinus wrote that "Inventions reached their limit long ago, and I see no hope for further development." The inaccuracy of his forecast is measured by the fact that the U.S. patent office currently grants about 100,000 patents per year.

Rising income is not the not the only way our living standards have improved: We also have more leisure time and better quality products to buy.

One hundred years ago, the average workweek was over sixty hours; today it's under forty. One hundred years ago, only 6% of manufacturing workers took vacations; today it's 90%. One hundred years ago, men entered the full-time labor force in their early teens; today labor force participation by young teenagers is essentially zero. One hundred years ago, only 26% of male workers retired by age sixty-five; today over 80% of sixty-five-year-old males have retired. One hundred years ago, the average housekeeper spent twelve hours a day on laundry, cooking, cleaning and sewing; today it's about four hours.

As for improvements in quality, try this experiment: Find yourself a twenty-five-year-old Sears catalogue. Correct the prices for inflation. (Prices have roughly tripled in the past twenty-five years.) Now ask whether you'd prefer to shop from that catalogue at those prices or from today's catalogue at today's prices. I guarantee you'll be *stunned* at how much better things have gotten in a mere quarter century.

Or, if you prefer, take a product like health care. Would you rather purchase, say, 1950-quality health care at 1950 prices, or today's quality health care at today's prices? I'll wager that virtually any well-informed consumer would choose the latter, which must mean that, despite all the hype about rising costs, health care is a better bargain today than it was in 1950.

The moral is that increases in measured income—even the phenomenal increases of the nineteenth and twentieth centuries—tend to understate improvements in our economic condition. The average middle-class American might have a smaller measured income than the European monarchs of the Middle Ages, but that does not prevent the American from leading a more luxurious lifestyle. It is not improbable that Henry VIII would have traded half his kingdom for modern plumbing, a lifetime supply of penicillin, and access to the Internet.

Will these trends continue? Of course, nobody knows—just as nobody knows whether the earth will be destroyed by an asteroid in ten years. But we can make educated guesses about probabilities. What we do know is that economic growth, despite some minor and temporary ups and downs, has continued pretty much unabated for the past two hundred years. We know also that all of that growth was fueled by technological progress. And we can reasonably conjecture that the reason we're not running out of fuel is that technological progress replenishes itself: Each new idea makes the next new idea easier to come by. Add to that Professor Kremer's argument that increasing wealth allows us to support a larger population, which in turn figures out new ways to create wealth, and there is excellent reason for optimism.

A skeptic could easily point to countries where large populations coexist with abysmal economic conditions.[2] But without exception, those are countries where the natural advantages of population size—a larger pool of geniuses and an abundance of trading partners—are undercut by government policies that limit both the rewards for ingenuity and the opportunities for trade. When the advantages of population growth are eliminated, only the disadvantages remain.[3]

And that's not all. A large population brings many blessings besides prosperity. We value our neighbors not just as potential trading partners, but as potential friends and potential mates. We value our children for reasons that have little to do with their earning capacity. A lot of people prefer New York to Montana, or Calcutta to the surrounding countryside, because there are advantages to living in a crowd.

---

2. A counter-skeptic could point to Hong Kong.

3. One could also argue that the populations of individual countries are not the relevant variables. Because anything that's invented in one place can easily be copied in other places, it could be only the *world* population that's important.

A world with more people is a world with more diversity. Chamber music, parasailing, and Ethiopian restaurants can survive only where the population is large enough to support them. In a less populated world, there wouldn't have been enough readers to justify publishing this book. I'd consider that unfortunate, and I hope that you would too.

I recently got a letter from a reader in Detroit who said that overpopulation had made his city unlivable. I refused to take him seriously because he chose to remain in Detroit—thereby revealing that, for him, the advantages of life in a population center continue to outweigh the disadvantages. Nobody has to live in a crowded place unless he wants to. Manhattanites will tell you that they stay in New York because of the theater or the symphony or the job opportunities—but that's just another way of saying that they stay in New York because it's crowded.

Thomas Malthus, that most dismal of scientists, welcomed the nineteenth century with a gloomy prophecy of uncontrolled population growth leading inexorably to mass starvation and human misery. It hasn't happened that way (at least not yet), and one reason it hasn't is that technological progress—fueled by the very population growth that Malthus so feared—has enabled food production to grow (and continue growing) at geometric rates. But Malthus's lack of vision goes much deeper than his failure to foresee the march of technology. There's something far more fundamental that he failed to perceive.

As you go through life, you claim a share of the world's resources—fish, petroleum, land, and a myriad of others. Malthus and his followers (up to the present day) have made the fundamental error of assuming that when you claim those resources, you slightly impoverish each of your neighbors. But that's not right. To see why not, think about exactly *how* you lay claim to those resources. Some you produce; that doesn't impoverish anyone. Some you trade for; that doesn't impoverish anyone either (you might take a fish from me, but I'll get something I value even more in return). The rest you inherit, and only then do you diminish someone else's share. But your inheritance does not take resources from humanity in general; it takes them from your siblings in particular.

That's a key point, and it's often missed. When people think about overcrowding or overpopulation, they typically imagine that if, for example, I had not been born, everyone else would have a slightly bigger share of the pie. The truth is that if I had not been born, both of my sisters would have substantially bigger shares of the pie and everybody else's share would pretty much the same as it is now.

That simple observation completely overturns Malthus, and here's why: It means that each family can choose its own population growth rate, and no family has to be impoverished by population growth unless it wants to be. If you and I each own a thousand acres, and if my family doubles its size every generation while yours practices zero population growth, then in ten generations my descendants will own less than an acre apiece, but yours will still own a thousand acres. My family's immoderate fertility is no concern of yours.[4]

Parents who love their children face a tradeoff: The more children you have, the less you can give to each of

---

4. In fact, if anything, your descendants will be grateful for all the cheap labor available to work their large plots of land.

them. Reasonable people disagree about how to resolve that tradeoff. Some find poverty an acceptable price to pay for a large family; others prefer fewer children with a higher living standard. That's not a conflict that needs to be resolved; it's an opportunity to celebrate diversity.

Professional alarmists demand that we ask how many people the earth can support. That's the wrong question. There's no need for you to worry how many people the earth can support; concentrate instead on how many people *your share* of the earth can support and calibrate your family size appropriately. If somebody else decides to stretch his share a little thinner, only a busybody would protest.

The day you were born, you brought both costs and benefits into this world. The costs include the demands you made (and continue to make) on the world's resources. The benefits include your ongoing contributions to the world's stock of ideas, love, friendship, and diversity.

I want to ask whether the costs exceed the benefits, or vice versa. In other words: Should the rest of us consider your birth (or any child's birth) a blessing or a curse?

Let's not try to settle this by listing all the costs and benefits of sharing the world with other people. Making lists is never conclusive, because you never know what you've overlooked. After an evening stuck in summer traffic, you'll remember that the driver in front of you imposed a cost, but you'll forget that the guy who invented car air conditioning conferred a benefit. You'll remember the shopper who fumbled with coupons and slowed down the checkout line, but you'll forget the kind stranger who helped you change a tire on a cold winter night. New Yorkers remember to complain about the crowds, but forget that without the crowds New York would be Cedar Rapids.

So instead of making lists, let's try to reconstruct what was on your parents' minds when they were deciding whether to conceive a child. What were their biases? Is it more likely that they were undercounting costs or undercounting benefits?

They're unlikely to have overlooked many costs, because the costs are concentrated in your own family: Your birth diverted resources (including tangibles like inherited land and intangibles like parental attention) away from your parents' other beloved children.

The benefits are more diffuse. The clearest benefit of your birth is that it brought your parents much joy; they didn't overlook that one. But the remaining benefits are spread far and wide. If you build a better mousetrap, millions will be in your debt. If all you do is smile, you'll still brighten thousands of days.

We don't know how to list those benefits, but we do know that a lot of them fall on total strangers, and your parents probably didn't think about them very much.

So when your parents were deciding whether to bring you into this world, they weighed most of the costs against only a small part of the benefits—and they *still* wanted you! From a broader social perspective—one that weighs *all* the costs and benefits—you must have been quite a bargain indeed.

The same argument applies to most children—excepting only those who impose substantial costs outside their own families by becoming thieves or major polluters. Most children are on net a good thing.

Here I want to insert a more systematic summary of the argument I've just made. If you're already convinced, you can skip this part.

Your birth brought costs and benefits to your family and to society at large. Here's what we know about those costs and benefits:

1. The benefits to society exceed the benefits to your family, because the benefits to society *include* the benefits to your family (which, after all, is part of society), as well as your contributions to the prosperity and happiness of others.
2. We can presume that according to your parents' calculations, the benefits to your family exceed the costs to your family; otherwise you wouldn't be here.
3. The costs to your family are approximately equal to the costs to society, because the major costs to society are in the form of resource consumption, and the resources you consume (except for those you produce and those you trade for) come from other members of your family.
4. Combining the first three points, we can infer that the benefits to society exceed the costs to society. And the same is true for every child born.[5]

---

5. The weakest link in this argument is point 3, for which there are significant exceptions such as the thieves and major polluters that I've already mentioned. But most people do not become thieves or major polluters. Other apparent "exceptions" are not what they seem. You might think, for example, that you impose costs on others when you bid up the price of cars or apply for a job that I was hoping to get. But these are not true costs, because they come packaged with offsetting benefits. When the price of cars goes up, sellers gain as much as buyers lose. If you prove a stronger job candidate than I am, my loss is the employer's gain.

I've argued that our children are on net a good thing. Now I want to argue that we don't have enough of them.

The key observation is the same as before: When parents are deciding whether to have a third, fourth, or fifth child, they are generally more conscious of the costs (which fall on them and their loved ones) than of the benefits (which are shared by many strangers).

When a decision maker is more conscious of costs than of benefits, he tends to make decisions that are overly conservative. That almost surely means that parents have fewer children than is socially desirable, and therefore the population grows too slowly.

Population growth is like pollution in reverse. The owner of a polluting steel mill weighs all its benefits (that is, his profits) against only a portion of its costs (he counts his expenses, but not the neighbors' health). Therefore he overproduces. Parents weigh all—or at least most—of the costs of an additional child (resources diverted from their other children) against only a portion of the benefits (they count their own love for their children, but not others' love for their children). Therefore they *under*produce.

To put this another way, it's always an occasion for joy when other people have more children: Those children just might enrich your life, and somebody else does all the work of raising them. That means we should be willing to subsidize each others' reproduction. In the absence of those subsidies we get too few children—just as in the absence of appropriate fines or taxes, we get too much steel.

Somewhere there is a young lady whose life has been impoverished by my failure to sire the son who would someday sweep her off her feet. If I cared as much about that young lady as I do about my own daughter, I'd have produced that son. But because I acted as if other people's children are less important than my own, I stopped reproducing too soon.

In other words, I was being selfish when I limited the size of my family. I understand selfishness. But I can't understand encouraging *others* to be selfish, which is the entire purpose of organizations like Zero Population Growth. It would make more sense to look for ways to subsidize reproduction. A world with many people is not only a more prosperous world; it is also a world that offers more potential friends who share our interests, more small acts of kindness between strangers, and a better chance of finding love. That's the kind of world we owe our children.

I've just argued that I should have had more children for the sake of strangers. A second, completely separate, argument says I should have had more children for the sake of those children themselves. Presumably they'd have been grateful for the gift of life.

I'm not sure how far to push that argument. There's no lack of public discussion about the rights of the unborn, but to evaluate the argument I've just put on the table, we have to go further and think about the rights of the un*conceived*. I don't expect an imminent consensus on either issue.

The following question seems to me to be both of supreme importance and supreme difficulty: Do living people have any moral obligation to the trillions of *potential* people who will never have the opportunity to live unless we conceive them?

The answer is surely either yes or no, but either answer leads to troubling conclusions. If the answer is yes, then it seems to follow that we are morally obligated to have more children than we really want. The unconceived are like prisoners being held in a sort of limbo, unable to break through into the world of the living. If they have rights, then surely we are required to help some of them escape.

Indeed, I've argued elsewhere that there can be no moral basis for trade policies or welfare policies that completely ignore the interests of non-Americans. By analogy, as long as the unconceived are moral entities, there can be no moral basis for reproductive policies that completely ignore the interests of the unconceived. That apparently bizarre conclusion is most easily avoided by rejecting the "yes" answer to the original question.

But if the answer is not yes, then it's no, and if the answer is no, then it seems there can be no moral objection to our trashing the entire earth, to the point where there will *be* no future generations. (That's not to say that we'd necessarily *want* to trash the earth; we might have selfish reasons for preserving it. It says only that if we ever *did* want to trash the earth, it would be morally permissible.)[6] If we prevent future generations from being conceived in the first place, and if the unconceived don't count as moral entities, then our crimes have no victims, so they're not true crimes.

This view is not unprecedented; Thomas Jefferson wrote that "the earth belongs to the living." Nor is it indefensible: If each of us individually has the right to forgo reproduction, then it's arguable that all of us collectively have that right. Nevertheless, stated this starkly, the conclusion does seem unsettling.

---

6. You'd have to modify this conclusion if you believe that animals (or for that matter plants!) have the kind of moral status that we're denying to unconceived humans.

When I first thought about this problem, I was extremely disturbed by the fact that both choices have implications that are difficult to embrace wholeheartedly, yet one or the other must be right. After considerable reflection, I lean to the view that the second one is right, though I can't prove it and I'm therefore not sure of it.

So if the unconceived have rights, we get one set of disturbing conclusions, and if they don't have rights we get a different set of disturbing conclusions. Perhaps there's a third way, and that's just to admit that we're incapable of being logically rigorous about issues involving the unconceived. Let me offer some evidence for that.

Surely you know couples like this: They already have two children, and they're undecided about whether to have a third. They waver back and forth; they lean one way and then the other; they weigh the pros and they weigh the cons. Finally they decide to go ahead. And from the instant that third child is born, the parents love it so deeply that they'd gladly sacrifice all their assets to preserve its life.

Compare that to the way people shop for appliances or furniture or compact disks. Ordinarily, the products you hesitate over are not the ones you end up treasuring most deeply. There are exceptions of course—sometimes that CD is surprisingly good once you get it home—but the general rule is that if you weren't sure you wanted it, it's unlikely to be cherished. Why, then, are children so different?

One of my colleagues maintains that there's no real inconsistency here. He says it's wrong to think of a baby as the equivalent of a microwave oven; instead you should think of it as the equivalent of an addictive drug. People hesitate about whether to try heroin; once they've decided to try it, they become addicted and can't give it up. Likewise with babies.

But that, I think, is a very bad analogy, because heroin addicts tend to be people who believed at the outset that they could escape addiction. Perhaps that's because they're foolish, or perhaps it's because they're high stakes gamblers, but that *is* what they were thinking. (Why else would we hear so many addicts recounting their experiences with the phrase "If only I had known . . ."?) That's not true of parents. Parents know in advance, and with near certainty, that they will be addicted to their children. They choose their addiction with eyes wide open, just like a customer choosing a microwave oven.

Moreover—and here is the key difference between parents and heroin addicts—parents know in advance, with near certainty, that they won't *want* to break their addiction. If you've already got two kids and are wavering over a third, then you've already got a pretty good idea what parenthood is like, and you already know that, unlike the addict who despises his addiction, you're going to *treasure* your attachment to your children. When you know you're going to love something that much after you've got it, how can you hesitate about getting it in the first place?

But as the parent of an only child, I can verify that people do behave that way. I know that my unconceived children would be my most valuable "possessions" if I brought them to fruition, yet I've chosen to leave them unconceived. Maybe there's just no logic here.

Let me leave you with one additional paradox. Suppose you're planning to conceive a child in the near future, and you're thinking about going down to the bank to purchase some bonds as a gift to that child. There is no doubt that the trip to the bank will cause a slight shift in your schedule for the rest of the day, hence a slight shift in the moment of conception, and hence a complete change in the identity of your child (because the sperm that's out in front of the pack at 10:01 is unlikely to be in front of the pack at 10:02).

Now, then: If you go to the bank, you will conceive child A, who is destined to be wealthy. If instead you spend all your money at the race track, you will instead conceive child B, who is destined to be poor. Moreover, you know in advance, based on the experience of virtually all parents, that no matter which child is born, that is the child you will prefer. If, twenty years after B is born, you were magically offered the opportunity to trade him for A, it's a sure bet that you wouldn't consider it. In fact, if an evil genie threatened to turn B into A, you'd pay him not to do it.

But by going to the bank instead of the racetrack, you are essentially *paying* for the privilege of siring the wealthy A instead of the impoverished B. This, despite the fact that you'd do practically anything to prevent B from turning into A after he's born. That seems very hard to reconcile with any economic theory of rational behavior, yet there it is.

All these paradoxes make it appear likely that nobody has yet invented a coherent way to think about the interests of the unconceived, or even about whether they *have* any interests. Ted Baxter longed for a creative genius who could solve the population problem; I'd settle right now for a creative genius who could teach us how to *think* about the population problem. I hope the next generation is large enough to include him.

The instant my daughter Cayley was born, my family's per capita income fell by one third. If per capita income is the right measure of human happiness, that must have been the worst moment of my life. But it didn't feel that way.

Economist Peter Bauer has pointed out that if per capita income is the right measure of human happiness, then the birth of a farm animal is a blessing and the birth of a child is a curse. But nobody thinks that way, because there is more to life than per capita income.

Other people—our friends and our children and sometimes even strangers who do us unexpected kindnesses—are among the luxuries that make life worth living. Most luxuries are expensive, and if children were expensive they'd be worth the price. But in a world where wealth flows from ideas, each child is born with with the prospect of making everyone more prosperous. Here is a luxury that pays for itself, and then some.

14

The Third R

Horace Mann is my hero.

Mann, the charismatic leader of the nineteenth century crusade for public schooling, is in disrepute among modern conservatives who suspect he cared less about education than about promoting communitarian ideals and stifling independent thought. In other words, they suspect that Mann would have been right at home among the professional educators of our own day. But it's hard to reconcile those suspicions with the reality of the man who wrote these words:

> Education is to inspire the love of truth, as the supremest good, and to clarify the vision of the intellect to discern it. We want a generation of men above deciding great and eternal principles, upon narrow and selfish grounds . . . . We want no men who will change, like the vanes of our steeples, with

> the course of the popular wind; but we want men who, like mountains, will change the course of the wind.
>
> . . . .
>
> Many,—may I not say most,—of those great questions, which make the present age boil and seethe, like a cauldron, will never be settled, until we have a generation of men who were educated, from childhood, to seek for truth and to revere justice. In the middle of the last century, a great dispute arose among astronomers, respecting one of the planets. Some, in their folly, commenced a war of words, and wrote hot books against each other; others, in their wisdom, improved their telescopes and soon settled the question forever. Education should imitate the latter.

Those impeccable sentiments have never been expressed more eloquently. Mann was wrong about some things—he was convinced, for example, that it takes a government to run an efficient school system—but regarding the purpose and methods of education his vision was never short of brilliant.

Mann firmly and consistently advocated teaching students *how* to think, rather than *what* to think. Here's his critique of rote learning:

> When lessons are given in this way the pupil, being unable to comprehend the ideas, tries to remember the words, and thus, as best, is sent away with a single fact, instead of a principle, explanatory of whole classes of facts. The lessons are learned by rote; and when a teacher practices upon the rote system, he uses the minds of the pupils, just as they use their own slates, in working arithmetical questions;—whenever a

second question is to be wrought, the first is sponged out, to make room for it.

Mann reports on a visit to an elementary school, where the students excelled at memorizing facts:

> A class of small scholars in geography, on being examined respecting the natural divisions of the earth,—its continents, oceans, islands, gulfs, etc.,—answered all the questions with admirable precision and promptness. Then they were asked, by their visitor . . . whether they had ever seen the earth about which they had been reciting; and they unanimously declared, in good faith, that they never had.

To a college teacher, that passage resonates with authenticity. You would be amazed how frequently we encounter students who simply do not understand that the material they are studying is supposed to be *about* something, and to make sense. Given a homework problem in economics, students will do simple calculations leading them to conclude that the price of lettuce is 80 cents a head at each individual grocery store, but 90 cents a head on average—and still believe that it's possible they've done the problem correctly. I recently assigned a problem where students were required to calculate the value of free toys distributed by Santa Claus, and a substantial fraction of the class reported *negative* numbers—with no apparent embarrassment. When I ask them to describe the effects of a $10,000 increase in Wrigley's labor costs, there are always students quick to respond that chewing gum prices will rise by $10,000 per pack.

These are not isolated incidents. They happen all the time. A good 20% of my students appear to have no recognition of the principle that when something doesn't make sense, you're supposed to question it.

I don't know who to blame. Maybe the students are just lazy; maybe I haven't figured out how to inspire them. But I'm betting that a substantial part of the problem originates in elementary school.

The product of a successful education is an intelligent skeptic—someone who cannot encounter a new "fact" without instinctively stopping to ask if it seems plausible. If the fact concerns something of sufficient importance, he or she will go beyond questioning its plausibility to investigating whether it is true.

Education means learning to ask "Is it plausible?" in an intelligent way. Often, this means finding the right thought-experiment. For example, it is sometimes said that Japanese car manufacturers make Americans worse off through the practice of "dumping" (selling cars for artificially low prices). Having been told such a thing, the successfully educated person might pause to consider whether the Japanese could make Americans worse off by giving every U.S. citizen a free Lexus. Having performed that thought-experiment, who can go on believing that dumping hurts Americans? Only those who got the wrong answer to my Santa Claus question.

In astronomy, many of the bitterest disputes are best resolved through the lens of a telescope. In public policy, many of the bitterest disputes are best resolved through the lens of arithmetic. I don't mean the grubby kind of arithmetic where you add up columns of numbers; I mean the simple conceptual kind of arithmetic where you notice that you if you spend more on one thing, then (as long as your income hasn't changed) you've got to spend less on something else.

For example, there are a lot of people who believe that Americans should invest more resources in high tech industries. But because those resources have to come from somewhere, a well educated skeptic will instinctively ask "Then in exactly which industries should we invest *fewer* resources?" (I don't mean to imply that there can't in principle be a perfectly adequate answer to that question, only that it needs to be asked.)

Another example: There is a widely held belief that because Americans spend more on health care than, say, Japanese or Canadians, it follows that Americans spend "too much." But Americans have higher incomes than Japanese and Canadians, so the laws of arithmetic require us to spend more than they do on *something* (unless of course we just throw part of our income away).[1] Therefore the appropriate question is this: If Americans should spend less on health care, what should they spend more on instead? Nintendo games?

Arithmetic, of course, is indispensable for making sense of large numbers. When somebody tells you that health care accounts for 14% of our $7 trillion GDP,[2] it's nearly impossible to envision what that means. That makes it easy for

---

1. You might want to object that Americans don't have to spend their entire incomes; they can always add to their savings instead. But the only reason to save is to spend even more in the future, so saving only postpones the inevitable spending.

2. GDP, or gross domestic product, is the total value of all income produced in the country in a given year.

demagogues to exaggerate its importance. But anyone with an instinct to calculate is immune from that kind of manipulation. If 14% of income goes to health care, then the average $50,000-a-year family spends about $7,000 a year on health-related expenses (including dental work, eyeglasses, and roughly $3,000 in tax payments for Medicare, Medicaid, and other medical expenditures by the government). Those are numbers that it's possible to think about, and that's a prerequisite for any reasonable discussion.

Here's what happens when people fail to account for the laws of arithmetic, or for the basic logic that underlies those laws: I've just been reading in the *Wall Street Journal* about a new kind of gall bladder surgery that originally promised to cut costs dramatically. Unfortunately (according to the *Journal*), the procedure has proved so popular, and is therefore performed so frequently, that total expenditures on gall bladder surgery have gone up instead of down. The *Journal* article concludes that as a means of cutting medical costs, the new procedure appears to be a failure.

By that logic, your $2,000 desktop computer is more expensive than the multimillion dollar mainframes of thirty years ago, because so many desktop computers are sold. By the same logic, grocery shoppers should be unhappy when the price of beef comes down and they choose to buy a lot more of it.

The *Journal* reporter made the elementary error of confusing the *price* of a good with the *expenditure* on that good. (Your expenditure on beef is the price per pound times the number of pounds you buy.) When the price falls, consumers are happier. If at the same time expenditure rises, that's because consumers *choose* to buy more beef. That free choice can't be a bad thing.

Likewise for surgery. If it's gotten cheaper to get your gall bladder fixed, that's a boon. If a lot more gall bladders are getting fixed as a result, that's an even bigger boon.

Here's an example of exactly the same mistake in a very different context: A few years ago, I wrote a book called *The Armchair Economist,* where I reported the fact (well known to economists) that when cars became safer in the 1960s (through seat belts, padded dashboards, etc.), drivers responded by becoming more reckless—so much so that the number of driver deaths stayed approximately constant. (Since that book was published, researchers have found similar effects for the safety improvements of the 1990s, like driver's side airbags and antilock braking systems.) Several book reviewers tried to infer that drivers don't benefit from seat belts. That's just wrong. The newly seat-belted driver might be just as likely as ever to get killed behind the wheel, but now he gets to drive more recklessly in the meanwhile. Drivers must value that opportunity to be more reckless, or they wouldn't choose to grab it.[3]

The explicit analogy is this: Putting on a seat belt lowers the *price* of reckless driving. When the price falls, people drive more recklessly—just as when the price of beef falls,

---

3. On the other hand, an increase in reckless driving means more danger to pedestrians. Given the gains to drivers and the losses to pedestrians, seatbelts might or might not be socially desirable on net.

people buy more beef. The number of driver deaths is like your total butcher bill—it can go up, down, or stay the same. But in any case, we can be sure that a fall in price makes consumers—or in this case drivers—better off.

Another recent *Journal* article concerned a traffic engineer who redesigns urban thoroughfares to create congestion and traffic jams—because he has noticed that areas with a lot of congestion tend to have a lot of good stores, theaters, and restaurants. This is akin to hanging mistletoe in July because you've noticed that in months when you hang mistletoe you tend to get a lot of presents. The fundamental error is to assume that when two things occur in tandem, the first must be the cause of the second. In the classroom, I have found that students who are good at mathematics—and hence good at thinking about the different ways in which variables can be related to each other—are immune to this kind of error. Those who aren't comfortable with math often fall into the error with remarkable ease. Fortunately, they can still get jobs as traffic engineers or *Wall Street Journal* reporters.

Several years ago there was a report that pipe smokers live longer, on average, than nonsmokers. I wonder how many traffic engineers took up pipe smoking in the expectation that it would make them live longer. Alas, it's far more probable that the causality runs in the opposite direction: It's not pipe smoking that causes longevity; it's longevity that causes pipe smoking. Most people don't take up the pipe until relatively late in life.

If that's not crystal clear, think about an extreme version of the same phenomenon: People who have heart attacks on their hundredth birthday live, on average, far longer than people who *don't* have heart attacks on their hundredth birthday. (In fact, every one of them lives to be at least one hundred.) But if today is your hundredth birthday, it does not follow that you can extend your life by giving yourself a heart attack.

Another example: It was reported several years ago that right-handed people live longer than left-handed people, by something like nine years on average. Many reporters jumped to the conclusion that right-handedness increases longevity. But an alternative explanation is that nearly everybody who is above a certain age was raised in an era when left-handers were forced to become right-handers. In that case, it's longevity that tends to cause right-handedness, not the other way around.

In all these examples, observers were led astray by a confusion between cause and effect. That's fundamentally a mathematical error—a failure to keep track of the proper relationships among variables. I have no doubt that junior high school students could successfully be trained to rid themselves of such confusions, via a course that would give them both the intellectual tools to think clearly about causality and the confidence to challenge unclear thinking wherever they encounter it. I'd like to see every eighth grader enrolled in such a course. I think Horace Mann would approve.

Just before the last presidential election, one of the Sunday morning news shows devoted half an hour to political prognostications. The first guest was a political scientist who had examined variables like the unemployment rate, the economic growth rate, and the number of U.S. troops on foreign soil. Historical experience told him how useful each variable would have been as a predictor of *past* elections, and he summarized this knowledge in what statisticians call a "regression equation." Then he used the equation to make a forecast.

The next guest was a historian who could barely contain his disgust. Using a mere equation to represent something as complex as a presidential election was, he said, reductionism carried past the point of absurdity. How, then, asked the host, would the historian go about forecasting an election? You'd have to consider a great number of things, answered the historian. You'd have to think about the unemployment rate, the economic growth rate, the number of U.S. troops on foreign soil . . . .

The historian, in other words, had no fundamental objection to what the political scientist had done. He objected only to the fact that the political scientist used an equation to keep careful *track* of what he had done.

What an odd opinion—that it's okay to do something in a vague and sloppy way but not okay to do exactly the same thing with a bit more care. Yet I'm sure the historian spoke for millions of viewers. There is a widespread hostility to quantification which seems to be based on nothing more than superstition or laziness of thought, and is, I think, one of the great failures of our educational system.

It is possible, perhaps, that the historian objected not to the political scientist's equation, but to the way the equation was presented; maybe he feared that it gave a false impression of precision. But that's a straw man: *nobody* believes that it's possible to write down an equation that predicts elections with precision; everybody understands that all predictions are based on limited past experience and that even some of that past experience might no longer be relevant. We're all groping in the dark, and we all know we're all groping in the dark; the only issue in dispute is whether we're going to grope carefully and systematically or just flail around for a while.

The irrational hostility to quantification can have a paralyzing effect on social institutions. Consider what happens in a criminal trial, where the judge instructs the jurors to convict if they believe the defendant is guilty "beyond a reasonable doubt," without telling them whether a "reasonable doubt" consists of 1% doubt, 2% doubt, or 5% doubt. (A 2% doubt means, for example, that if the jurors sat on 100 cases with equally strong evidence, they'd expect 98 of the defendants to be guilty.) Lawyers scoff at the notion that doubt can be quantified so precisely. Their scoffing is justified but irrelevant. It is true that no juror can be sure whether his doubt is more or less than 2%, but it is equally true that no juror can be sure whether his doubt is more or less than "reasonable." With a quantified target, jurors would at least know what to aim for, even if they can't be sure of hitting it.[4]

Why do judges systematically conceal what they are thinking of when they use the phrase "reasonable doubt"? Partly, perhaps, it's to keep jurors off balance and dependent on the judge for continual guidance. A better educated jury pool wouldn't stand for it.

---

4. Another advantage of quantification is that it would give legislators the flexibility to set different standards for different crimes.

Around Cayley's third birthday, I took her out for a very long stroll in the neighborhood of the Colorado State University campus, where we were living at the time. When we got around to the far end of campus—an area I'd not explored with her before—she started telling me that she had gone to see some stuffed dead animals somewhere near here. I asked her who took her, and she said she'd gone with her lab school. (It later turned out that the field trip with the lab school had been six months earlier. Some memory!)

I thought I knew where to find these stuffed dead animals, so I asked if she'd like to see them again. Much excitement. Unfortunately, I was wrong about where they were. So we wandered from building to building for a very long time, asking people and not getting much information.

Finally someone suggested the zoology department and we started off in that direction. It turned out I didn't know where that was either. After a while I asked a passerby for directions to zoology and got them. Cayley was very excited that this man had known the way, and commented on it several times. She also warned me repeatedly that the animals are in a building where you have to be very quiet—undoubtedly a lab school legacy.

When we got to the building, she said in hushed amazement "I was here before!" We found a spot among the birds and the mammals, where she sat for long minutes in quiet meditation. Finally she whispered, "He just thought about it . . . and then he knew where it was." She was witness to a miracle.

In the dim silence of a one-room museum, Cayley sat bewitched, not by the eyes of owls and tigers but by the grandeur of pure thought. We lingered for a while and then she was ready to leave.

In the next three chapters, I want to illustrate Cayley's greatest discovery—that thinking can get you where you want to go.

More particularly, I want to illustrate how a little bit of mathematics can get you a long way toward the calm resolution of a hotly disputed issue. The issues I've chosen are the consequences of government debt, the existence of racial discrimination, and the nature of our obligations to future generations. They are arranged in increasing order of mathematical sophistication. The first two are pretty straightforward; the last is somewhat more demanding.

The three examples illustrate three different kinds of mathematical reasoning. In the first, on government debt, a sample calculation illustrates a general principle in a way that is quite simply irrefutable, although it appears to be very poorly understood by people who have not studied economics. The numbers in the sample calculation are entirely fictional, but it's clear from the arithmetic that the argument works equally well regardless of the numbers you choose.

In the second example, on racial discrimination, a rough back-of-the-envelope calculation with some realistic numbers casts doubt on the plausibility of some widely held beliefs. The result is not an irrefutable proof, but a strong indication of what's probable.

The third example is about using mathematics to keep track of the consequences of our ethical preconceptions. As I said, it's probably harder to follow than the first two. If you're not feeling energetic, you might want to skip it.

15

The Arithmetic of Government Debt

IF YOU ARE WORRIED THAT GOVERNMENT debt hurts your grandchildren, then I can show you some arithmetic to set your mind at ease. You'll learn a lot if you follow this example:

Suppose you have $1,000 in the bank, where it will double by the time your grandchildren inherit it.

Now suppose the government decides to spend $100 of your money. It has two options for acquiring that $100.

Option A: Raise your taxes by $100. That leaves you $900, which will double so that your grandchildren inherit $1,800.

Option B: Borrow the $100. That leaves you $1,000, which will double so that your grandchildren will inherit $2,000. At that point, the government must tax your grandchildren $200 to repay its debt with interest. That leaves your grandchildren $1,800.

There are two morals here. First, government spending is costly to your grandchildren. If it weren't for the spending, they'd end up with $2,000 instead of $1,800. Second, the choice between options A and B is of no consequence to your grandchildren at all. The "balanced budget" option—option A—leaves your grandchildren neither better nor worse off than the "deficit spending" option—option B.

In other words, it is simply not true that government debt hurts your grandchildren—at least as long as you care enough about them to leave them a bequest. In other words, government *debt* (as opposed to government *spending*) can't hurt your grandchildren unless you want it to.

That's not fancy economic theory; it's simple arithmetic. It's not controversial among economists, and it's not controversial among the numerically literate. It is, however, immensely controversial among the sort of people who adamantly refuse to work through a simple calculation before jumping to conclusions.

Such people are legion. I know this because I presented the simple arithemetic in a magazine column not long ago, and I got about 150 letters from readers who refused to accept it. A few of those letters were refreshingly insightful. But most were from people who insisted—with incredible tenacity, through multiple rounds of correspondence—that the conclusion was wrong, *even though they made no attempt to point to any error in the reasoning.*

I find it both sad and frightening when people go on believing what they want to believe even in the face of conclusive arguments to the contrary which they cannot refute. At the very least, I would expect them to feel some sense of vague discomfort about that. I'm disturbed not just because they reject this particular argument, but because they seem to believe there's nothing to be learned from careful arguments in general. It's clear from their letters that most of them never even read the arithmetic. Instead, they tried to change the subject.

For example, an amazing number of people (typically members of the Concord Coalition, an organization dedicated to the advancement of hysteria about fiscal matters) wrote to tell me how big the national debt is, apparently missing the point that the same argument works whether the government spends $1 or $100 or $1,000. I wrote back to every one of them, asking exactly which step in my arithmetic they found objectionable. Most of them responded by reiterating that the national debt is really, really big.

One gentleman wrote to express his outrage that the government can borrow as much as it does. "My kids can't do it, my wife can't do it, my business can't do it; why should the government be able to do it?," he asked me.

Well, neither your wife nor your kids nor your business can raise taxes either. If the government's going to spend your money, it's got to get it either through borrowing or through taxes and *either way* it's exceeding the powers of your wife, your kid, and your business.[1] When I said as much in reply, my correspondent got the point, and said he'd never thought of it that way before. Now he saw the issue in a whole new light.

---

1. There is a third alternative: Instead of borrowing or raising taxes, the government could spend less. That's an alternative I can get enthusiastic about. But both my correspondent and I were taking the level of government spending as given, and debating only whether the burden of that spending is magnified when it is financed by borrowing.

Now, I don't want to be too hard on an attentive and open-minded reader, but I am utterly baffled as to how thoughtful adults can mouth platitudes like "my wife can't, my children can't, my business can't" without stopping to ask themselves exactly what the "can't" applies to. The right answer is not that your wife, children, and business can't borrow, but that they can't spend other people's money. For better or worse, that's something the government does routinely.

If your argument is "my wife can't borrow as the government does, so the government should fund its spending through taxes instead of borrowing," I'll respond: "Well, *my* wife can't raise taxes as the government does, so the government should fund its spending through borrowing instead of taxes." My argument's no better than yours, but it's no worse either.

If the wife-and-children argument had been confined to this one exchange from my personal correspondence, I wouldn't take up so much space on it here. But I have seen and heard this argument dozens of times, in op-ed pieces and on Sunday morning television, from politicians and from journalists. My point is not simply that it's wrong, but that it's so fundamentally wrong that it can succeed only when people mouth the words without ever stopping to think about what they mean.

Then there were the people who wrote to tell me that government borrowing is of course justifiable when it funds productive investments, but not when it funds wasteful spending. I assume they were repeating some garbled version of something they'd heard in a college business class. There's the power of education for you; these were the correspondents who most adamantly refused to see the point no matter how many times I wrote back to them. And to be explicit, here's the point they were missing: The option A/option B scenarios apply equally well regardless of what the government spends your $100 on.

Finally, there were the people who wanted to analogize the government to a large corporation like AT&T, with the citizens as the shareholders. Just as AT&T shareholders are happy when AT&T runs a surplus, they reasoned, so U.S. citizens should be happy when the U.S. government runs a surplus.

What these writers tended to overlook is that the U.S. government is not *exactly* like a large corporation. It's much more like a large corporation *with the power to tax its shareholders.* If AT&T were allowed to tax its shareholders, it could run an enormous surplus—but the shareholders might be disinclined to celebrate. (Nor would they necessarily be much inclined to complain; their shares would increase in value by the amount they'd paid in taxes.) Likewise, when the government reduces its deficit by raising taxes, don't expect dancing in the streets.

Along the Pacific Coastal Highway, just south of Big Sur, there's a place called Jade Cove. It's a place of spectacular beauty, even by the standards of that spectacularly beautiful part of the world. You can pull to the side of the road and climb down 300 feet to a rocky beach littered with jade, constantly replenished by the sea. As the tide rises, rolling waves submerge the beach so that you have to climb up on the rocks to stay dry.

Cayley exults in the beauty and the challenge of Jade Cove. From her high perch, she waits for the waves to recede, then hops down to claim a special treasure and scrambles back up just ahead of the incoming breakers. Usually, she makes it. When she doesn't, she's sure to be knocked flat and almost sure to come up laughing.

You have to be careful where you store your belongings on the beach at Jade Cove. If they're not high enough, the more powerful waves can snatch them out to sea.

Now I want you to imagine this scenario: Cayley and I have climbed down to the beach and left our identical windbreaker jackets next to each other on a rock. I've climbed up to a ledge safely above the waterline and stayed dry. Cayley has collected a pocketful of jade and spent some serious time under water. I'm warm and she's cold. It's time to go. Only now do we notice that the sea has extracted a price for Cayley's treasures: her windbreaker is gone. Mine, by chance, remains.

As I put on my jacket and we start the long climb up to the car, I look at my poor freezing child and wish that there was something I could do for her. If only the sea had taken my jacket instead of hers, I'd feel so much better.

Halfway up, we meet another traveler—let's say you—and share our tale of woe, explaining that our luck was doubly bad. Not only did we lose a jacket, we lost the *wrong* jacket. Cayley needs hers much more than I need mine.

Are you inclined to sympathize? Or are you more inclined to suggest that I give Cayley my jacket?

The story of Jade Cove contains everything you need to know about the national debt. The government is like the waves—it rolls in, bringing gifts (of jade or of medicare benefits) and exacting a price (in jackets or in taxes). Like the waves, the government can act capriciously. Sometimes it takes from us (as when it increases our taxes); other times it takes from our children (as when it increases the debt).

It can make good sense to complain that the government is taking too much—just as it can make good sense to wish the waves had been gentler and left both jackets on the beach. But it is silliness to complain that the government took from your children when it should have taken from you.

A father who sincerely wishes that the sea had taken his own jacket instead of his daughter's can rectify the problem by giving her his jacket. A parent who sincerely wishes that the government had raised his own taxes instead of his childrens' can rectify the problem by giving them money to pay their taxes with—typically by adding it to their bequests.

A commentator who says "Government debt allows me to live better at my children's expense" might be telling the truth—just like a father who says "The whims of the sea allow me to stay warm while my daughter freezes." Such statements can be true for some of the people some of the time—namely, the sort of people who won't give a jacket to a freezing child (or the sort of people who think that their children aren't really freezing).

But a commentator who says "Government debt allows me to live better at my children's expense *and I don't like that*" is always lying—just like a father who says "The whims of the sea allow me to stay warm while my daughter freezes *and I don't like that.*" Such statements are false for all of the people all of the time. A genuinely unhappy father would give away his jacket and a genuinely unhappy commentator would increase his bequest.

That powerful analogy suggests correctly that the "burden" of government debt is something you can easily remove from the backs of your children. The only sure way to verify that the analogy is accurate is to see whether it survives the test of translation to arithmetic. That was exactly the purpose of working through options A and B.

Are you tempted to respond that you'd *like* to leave an extra $100 to your grandchildren but you don't have the money? If so, you should be strongly in *favor* of government debt. Here's why: If the government doesn't borrow, it has to raise your taxes. If you really don't have money to leave to your grandchildren, then you won't have money to pay those taxes with either. So for you, the alternative to government debt is a jail term.

More generally, the whole point is that government debt keeps your taxes lower than they would otherwise be, and those tax savings provide the resources for you to give your grandchildren. Sometimes people fail to follow this argument because they get confused about the role of interest payments. They think that the choice is between a $100 tax bill for you or a $110 tax bill for the next generation, and that the latter is $10 more expensive. That's wrong, because you only have to put aside $100 today in order to pay that future tax bill—your savings grow while the next generation is waiting to inherit them.

At the beginning of this chapter, I worked out the arithmetic of government debt on the assumption that you care enough about your grandchildren to leave a bequest. In that case, government debt makes no difference to your granchildren.

Now let's figure out what happens if you *don't* care enough about your grandchildren to leave a bequest (Of course in this case you also won't care enough about your grandchildren to complain about the national debt!) To do that, let's revisit options A and B. Assume again that you have $1,000 in the bank, but this time assume you plan to spend every penny and leave no inheritance. Once again, suppose the government decides to spend $100 of your money.

Here are the options:

Option A: Raise your taxes by $100. That leaves you $900 to spend, and your grandchildren will be born debt-free.

Option B: Borrow the $100. That leaves you $1,000 to spend, and your grandchildren will be born $100 in debt.

In this case, the debt certainly hurts your grandchildren. So the new moral is this: The debt can enrich you at the expense of your grandchildren, but only if you want it to. If you care enough to leave an inheritance, the inheritance grows along with the government debt. If you *don't* care enough to leave an inheritance, your grandchildren have a problem.

Finally, a question of greater subtlety. Suppose you care about your grandchildren but I don't care about mine. When the government increases its debt, it takes money from our grandchildren and gives it to us. You don't like that, so you return the money to your grandchildren through a bequest. I like it just fine, so I go on a spending spree. The new question is: Can *my* spending spree hurt *your* grandchildren?

Well, it certainly can't hurt them nearly as much as if *you* went on a spending spree, so this is a question of secondary importance. But it's still worth addressing.

Here's the answer: Because of my spending spree, my grandchildren will have fewer resources. If, for example, they turn out to be factory owners, they'll have to make do with smaller factories.

How does that affect *your* grandchildren? It depends. It probably hurts them if they come to my grandchildren looking for a job. But it probably helps them if they own a competing factory. So my profligacy is bad for some of my neighbor's grandchildren but good for others.

The national debt is to the 1990s as the nuclear freeze was to the 1980s: It's the issue that you don't have to really understand before you can start feeling morally superior to your neighbors. From that point of view it's even better than the nuclear freeze; not only does your expression of deep concern put you on the moral high ground, but you actually get to stand on that ground and prescribe suffering for everybody else.

Here's a translation to adult-speak of something I try to tell my daughter from time to time: The impulse to moral smugness is unattractive but perhaps unavoidable. The best thing to do with it is to harness it for good. If you must feel superior to people, earn the right by first *analyzing* an issue (in this case starting with simple numerical examples); then stake your claim to the high ground not on the basis of your passion but of your understanding.

16

The Arithmetic of Discrimination

WHY DO BLACKS EARN LESS THAN WHITES do? The easiest hypothesis is that employers discriminate. I want to ask whether that hypothesis is really plausible. In the process, I want to demonstrate that when it comes to resolving this kind of controversy, a little bit of arithmetic can go a long way.

Some conservative commentators have attempted to dismiss the employer-discrimination hypothesis by noting that discrimination is costly (because it entails a willingness to pay premium wages for white workers) and therefore unattractive to employers with an eye on the bottom line.

But that dismissal is far too glib, because it assumes that employers never stray from the rational pursuit of profits. Equally simplistic theories predict (falsely) that employers never engage in nepotism and corporate executives never goof off on the golf course.

What is missing here is an estimate of *how* costly it is to discriminate. If discrimination costs employers 5% of their profits, it might survive—just as nepotism survives. If discrimination costs ten times that, it's less likely to be viable.

I want to provide the missing cost estimate, starting with a few assumptions that are reasonably commensurate with reality. First, I'll suppose that blacks constitute 10% of the workforce. Second, I'll suppose that blacks earn 60% of what whites earn. Third, I'll make an assumption (again guided by real world observations) about what happens to corporate revenue: I'll assume that for every dollar paid to the workers, a half a dollar gets paid to the bondholders and the stockholders collectively—let's say the bondholders and the stockholders each get a quarter.

To make those assumptions more concrete, suppose you are the manager of a corporation that employs one black and nine whites, paying the black $60,000 and the whites $100,000 apiece. That makes your total wage bill $960,000. The bondholders and the stockholders each receive one fourth as much as the workers, or $240,000 each.[1] So your payouts look like this:

9 white workers @ $100,000	$900,000
1 black worker @ $60,000	60,000
Bondholders	240,000
Stockholders	240,000
Total	$1,440,000

1. The specific numbers in this paragraph don't matter. If you assume 100 employees instead of 10, or wages of $6,000 and $10,000 instead of $60,000 and $100,000, the conclusions to follow will remain unaffected.

Now let's suppose that the black/white wage differential results from pure discrimination—that is, let's suppose that blacks are paid less even though blacks and whites are equally productive—and estimate the cost of that discrimination.

The numbers reveal two truths. First, discrimination must be quite common throughout the industry; otherwise your black employee would have moved to a nondiscriminating firm long ago. Second, if you could put aside your racism and focus solely on the bottom line, you'd replace your nine $100,000 whites with nine equally productive $60,000 blacks.[2] That would cut your wage bill by $360,000 (from $960,000 to $600,000).

Where do the $360,000 savings go? The same place any corporate savings go—into the pockets of the stockholders. The stockholders' earnings increase 150% (from $240,000 to $600,000) overnight. Your payouts now look like this:

10 black workers @ $60,000	600,000
Bondholders	240,000
Stockholders	600,000
Total	$1,440,000

When the return to stockholders rises by 150%, so must the price of your company's stock. That's enough to put you on the cover of *Time* magazine as the financial genius

2. It won't be hard to find those nine blacks, because we've already agreed that blacks must be suffering from discrimination throughout the industry. Surely you can lure nine of them to your own firm by offering just slightly more than the going black wage of $60,000.

of the century. To continue discriminating is to throw away an opportunity for unprecedented financial success.

In fact, that same opportunity is available to every other corporate manager in the industry as well, and they're rejecting it too (remember that discrimination must be widespread or all blacks would move to nondiscriminatory firms). So in order to believe that discrimination explains the black/white wage differential, you must believe that managers throughout the industry are so blinded by racism that they are willing to throw away a 150% gain for their stockholders, and the acclaim of all Wall Street for themselves. Personally, I find that wildly implausible.

The figure of 150% is based on numerical assumptions that are reasonable, but not ironclad. If you juggle those initial assumptions a bit, you'll get a number other than 150% coming out at the end, and you might or might not discover a scenario in which discrimination is plausible. (My guess is that you won't, but then again, you and I might have different standards for what's plausible.) Regardless of how that experiment turns out, it's well worth performing. Without some such test, there is simply no way to know whether discrimination is a credible hypothesis.

Let's be clear on what it takes to believe in employer discrimination, given the results of that calculation. Not only do you have to believe that *some* corporate managers are discarding a spectacular profit opportunity; you have to believe that *all* corporate managers—or at least all those who continue to employ a substantial number of whites—are discarding similar opportunities.

You might want to object that the profit opportunity is an illusion, because if managers tried to respond to it, they'd bid black wages up to the white level and the opportunity would disappear. But that doesn't explain why the opportunity remains unclaimed. If I leave $20,000 on a New York street corner, it will disappear very quickly; that's hardly a reason to predict that nobody will pick it up.

I've argued that discrimination is implausibly costly. But suppose I'm wrong. Suppose that racism is so deeply ingrained that vast numbers of corporate managers are willing to pay its price.

Suppose at the same time that you are one of the few corporate managers who overcomes that ingrained prejudice and hires an all-black workforce at $60,000. Are you still discriminating? Some would say yes, because you are paying blacks $60,000 to do a $100,000 job. Others would say no, because your hiring practices are motivated not by racial animus but by a profit opportunity created elsewhere in the market.

That argument seems to me to be largely about semantics, and probably unresolvable. But here is something we can agree on: No matter *how* you define discrimination, hiring blacks at $60,000 is surely less discriminatory than *refusing* to hire blacks at $60,000. And, again no matter how you define discrimination, the bottom line is this: If you are willing to discriminate less than everyone else, you end up with lots of black executives and a $360,000 profit for your shareholders; whereas if you discriminate as much as, or more than, everyone else, that profit opportunity is thrown away. So discrimination is heavily punished in the marketplace.

Who are the big losers from discrimination? You might think it's the black employees who are denied suitable positions. But it's also the stockholders who are denied the services of those black employees. In fact, the stockholders tend to lose a lot more than the employees do. In this example, for every black executive who can claim that discrimination costs him $40,000, there is a set of stockholders who can claim that discrimination costs them $360,000, or nine times as much.

When corporate managers indulge their personal tastes for Van Gogh oil paintings at a multimillion dollar cost to the stockholders, nobody has any trouble recognizing that the stockholders are being plundered. When those same managers indulge their personal tastes for racial discrimination at a multimillion dollar cost to the stockholders, the stockholders are victimized in a precisely analogous way.

You might want to argue that stockholders have a responsibility to keep an eye on the management's behavior, and they pay a legitimate cost for their failure to do so. But if the stockholders could keep an eye on everything that goes on around the corporation, they wouldn't need to hire managers in the first place. The managers' job is to earn profits for the stockholders, and if they throw away opportunities to do so, then the stockholders have been robbed.

I believe the magnitude of that robbery is so great as to make it very hard to imagine that it could be occurring in the first place; in other words, black/white wage differentials must have some explanation that does not involve discrimination. But if I'm wrong about that—if discriminaton *is* a significant phenomenon—then it's the stockholders more than the employees who merit our sympathy.

When the management of a large corporation is accused of racial discrimination, civil rights groups sometimes call on consumers to boycott the corporation's products. But the problem with boycotts is that they lower corporate profits, which punishes not the management but the stockholders—that is, not the sinners, but their primary victims. Likewise, compensatory payments to black employees are cruelly ironic, as they come from the pockets of those same, now doubly victimized, stockholders.

In 1996, the management of Texaco confessed to having discriminated in hiring and promotion, and agreed to compensate black employees to the tune of $176 million. That doesn't prove that Texaco discriminated; it might just mean that a false confession and a quick payoff seemed cheaper and easier than a protracted battle in the courts and the media. But if the confession was sincere and the $176 million was merited, then there should also have been a commensurate payment to the stockholders—not from corporate coffers, but from the personal assets of the managers who bilked their investors by failing to hire the best bargains in the labor market.

If we rule out employer discrimination, there must be some other explanation for the black/white wage differential.

Suppose, for example, that there is discrimination not by employers but by customers, who are willing to pay a premium for goods and services produced by white workers.

To advocate that theory convincingly, you'd have to estimate the size of the premium and assess whether it's something that consumers would plausibly pay. I invite readers to do their own arithmetic.

(The size of a plausible premium varies a lot from industry to industry. In computer hardware, it's hard to imagine that there could be any premium at all, because workers are essentially invisible to consumers—do you know the race of the person who assembled your disk drive? In barbering, you might expect a bigger premium, but that's not so clear, because even if there are a lot of racist customers, black barbers might still be able to specialize in serving nonracists. In major league baseball, however, where the players are both very visible and unable to pick and choose their fans, there's much greater potential for discrimination. And indeed, there's some evidence that the potential is fulfilled: Black major leaguers generally outperform white major leaguers, suggesting that the threshhold for promotion to the majors is set higher for blacks than for whites.)

Yet another theory is that blacks earn less because of discrimination not by employers or customers, but by their fellow workers. According to this theory, blacks are worth less because they sow discontent among the whites who have to work with them. But if this theory were true, you'd expect employers to avoid the problem by hiring racially homogeneous workforces—all black at some firms and all white at others.

An alternative theory is that blacks earn less because they have fewer marketable skills. There are two versions of this theory. The first version says that each worker is paid according to his individual skills, and blacks have (on average) fewer skills than whites do. The second version says that each worker is paid according to a reasonable *expectation* of his skills, and employers (correctly and reasonably) expect blacks to have fewer skills than whites do. According to the first version, a highly skilled black is paid as much as a highly skilled white; according to the second version, the highly skilled black is paid less, though for reasons that have nothing to do with racism.

Either version of this theory needs to be embellished with an explanation of *why* blacks have fewer marketable skills. The candidates are choice, training, and heredity.

"Choice" means that for some reason blacks voluntarily acquire fewer skills than whites do. (This might be rational if blacks expect to be discriminated against in the labor market; thus the effects of choice could magnify the effects of discrimination.) But that story seems inconsistent with some important evidence. According to recent research by Derek Neal of the University of Chicago and William Johnson of the University of Virginia, black/white wage differentials are largely explained by differences in skill levels which are already detectable at an early age. (Richard Herrnstein and Charles Murray had previously reported similar findings in their bestselling book *The Bell Curve*.) That's consistent with rational choice only if six-year-olds carefully consider their future employment prospects before deciding whether to master the multiplication table. I am devoted to rational choice models, but I'm not prepared to cross over from devotion to fanaticism.

That leaves two possible explanations for the black/white wage gap: training and heredity. (More precisely, these are explanations for the skill gap that causes the wage gap.)[3] Herrnstein and Murray argued that heredity plays a substantial role, but the more recent findings of Neal and Johnson tend to refute that interpretation. For one thing, Neal and Johnson report that on standardized intelligence tests, the performance gap between blacks and whites is considerably larger for young adults than it is for teenagers. That's hard to explain if the gap is caused by heredity (why should an inherent difference in intelligence become larger over time?),[4] but not if it's caused by training (if blacks get inferior schooling, then it's not surprising that the effects are greater after ten years of schooling than after six).

Much research remains to be done, and is being done, and will be done. All of that research, at least when it is useful, will be quantitative in one way or another. Some of it requires sophisticated techniques and sophisticated measurements. But there are cases—and discrimination is one of them—where the inherent plausibility of a theory can be well tested with nothing more than the back of an envelope and an open mind.

---

3. The relationship between skills and wages is strong but fairly recent. It's only in the past couple of decades that the job market has begun paying a substantial premium for the sorts of skills that are measured by standardized tests. Nobody's sure what caused the change, though the obvious guesses tend to invoke phrases like "silicon revolution."

4. Indeed, Herrnstein and Murray rest a substantial part of their argument on the assertion that these test scores measure inherent abilities that are not affected by training—but Neal and Johnson's research casts significant doubt on that assertion.

17

The Arithmetic of Conservation

WHAT DO WE OWE TO FUTURE generations?

It's of course impossible to answer that question without facing up to a more general question: What does anybody owe to anybody?

One possible answer is embodied in the economist's version of the Golden Rule: We should be willing to spend a dollar whenever it does more than a dollar's worth of collective good.

According to the Golden Rule, if we can spend a dollar to preserve a forest that will be worth a penny to each of the next 101 generations, that's desirable.

Unfortunately, if we're selfish, we might not spend that dollar—for two reasons. First, we can't charge admission fees to generations not yet born, so we might not care that they're willing to pay a penny each to get in. But that problem can be solved: As long as future owners will be able to collect those pennies, they are reflected in the forest's current price. That's because each future owner has to buy the forest from a previous owner, who takes account of its resale value when he decides what he's willing to pay for it.

The second problem lies deeper. Suppose, just for illustration, that generations are spaced a year apart, and the interest rate is 4% per year. Then the forest will sell for a quarter. Why? Because the forest returns a penny a year in admission fees, and the quarter returns a penny a year in interest. That makes the forest worth just as much as the quarter—no more, no less. But nobody will be willing to spend a dollar to preserve a forest that sells for only a quarter. The Golden Rule calls for conservation, but the profit motive undercuts the Golden Rule.

Whenever there's a positive interest rate, not enough forests get preserved—at least if the Golden Rule is your criterion for what's worth preserving. The higher the interest rate, the worse the problem. (If the interest rate were 10%, the forest would be worth only a dime, because then a dime would return the same penny a year that the forest does. In that case, nobody would spend more than a dime to preserve the forest.)

But maybe the Golden Rule is the wrong criterion. After all, the Golden Rule implies that if I can spend a dollar to do something for Bill Gates that he values at $1.01, I'm obligated to do it. Many people would absolve me of that obligation, because $1.01 is worth less to Bill Gates than a dollar is to me. In other words, many people don't believe that you should apply the Golden Rule when there are differences in wealth.

The question then becomes: What rule should we apply instead? To think about that, we need to quantify the crucial difference between me and Gates: Is a dollar to Gates the same as 90 cents to me? 50 cents? a dime? a half a penny?

Here are some hypotheses one could make:

Hypothesis 1: The value of a dollar is inversely proportional to your wealth. Thus when you are twice as rich, a dollar is worth half as much; when you are three times as rich, a dollar is worth a third as much, etc.

Hypothesis 2: The value of a dollar is inversely proportional to the *square* of your wealth. Thus when you are twice as rich, a dollar is worth one fourth as much; when you are three times as rich, a dollar is worth one ninth as much, etc.

Hypothesis 3: The value of a dollar is inversely proportional to the *cube* of your wealth. Thus when you are twice as rich, a dollar is worth one eighth as much, when you are three times as rich, a dollar is worth one twenty-seventh as much, etc.

And so forth.

We can get a pretty good idea which hypothesis is correct by looking at the kinds of risks people are willing to take. If the correct hypothesis is low on the list, people will take substantial risks in hope of winning substantial rewards; if the correct hypothesis is higher on the list, people will be more cautious.

The bulk of available evidence—from the way people behave in insurance markets, for example—indicates that the correct hypothesis is somewhere between 1 and 5; 10 is considered about the upper limit of what's plausible. The only exception is in financial markets, where people's willingness to hold bonds instead of stocks—despite the enormously superior performance of stocks in the long run—appears to reflect a degree of risk aversion that requires something like Hypothesis 30.[1] On balance, it's reasonable to assume something like Hypothesis 3.

To apply all this to the problem of forest preservation, we have to figure out how rich our descendants will be. It's reasonable to assume that per capita income (corrected for inflation) will grow at about 1.5% per year (this might be a bit low by historical standards; 2% would be a bit high). In that case, people born a year from now will be 1.5% richer than you and so (assuming Hypothesis 3) will value a dollar about 4.5% less than you do.[2]

(A word of warning: Ordinarily, when people talk about the falling value of a dollar, they're talking about inflation. The present discussion has nothing to do with that. Here the value of a dollar falls because people get richer. The 4.5% drop in value is over and above any change due to inflation.)

Given those numbers, a reasonable modification of the Golden Rule says that it's worth spending a dollar to preserve the forest only if it's worth at least 4.5 cents a year to future generations. That's just another way of saying that

---

1. $1,000 invested seventy years ago would be worth about $13,000 today if invested in bonds or about $850,000 if invested in stocks. The fact that it requires Hypothesis 30 to explain bondholding, while Hypothesis 5 is sufficient for almost any other risk-related behavior, is a paradox that economists call the *equity premium puzzle*.

2. Here's how I calculated that: Next year's child will have 1.015 times your income, and so—given Hypothesis 3—will value a dollar at $1 / (1.015)^3$ times what you do. That's about a 4.5% difference.

we're not required to sacrifice a dollar for something that future generations will collectively value at less than a dollar.

But if the inflation-adusted interest rate is, say, 4%, then profit seekers will spend a dollar to preserve any forest that returns more than 4 cents every year. If there are forests that return more than 4 cents but less than 4.5 cents, then too *many* forests get preserved. In this case, the profit motive leads us to do *more* than enough for future generations.

In general, write r for the interest rate (corrected for inflation, so that if bonds pay 7% and the inflation rate is 3%, then $r = 4\%$). Write g for the growth rate of per capita income (again corrected for inflation, so that g is probably between 1.5 and 2). Write s for the number of the true Hypothesis about risk aversion (probably between 1 and 5). Then if $r > g \cdot s$, profit-maximizing entrepreneurs will conserve too little, but if $r < g \cdot s$, profit-maximizing entrepreneurs will conserve too much.

Of course "too little" and "too much" here are to be interpreted in light of the ethical mandates of the modified Golden Rule—the one that says we should account for the fact that a forest is worth less to a rich man than a poor one.

The mathematics doesn't tell us whether the modified Golden Rule is the right ethical standard, but it does spell out the consequences of this or any other ethical standard we care to apply. In other words, the mathematics keeps us ethically honest. That's no small matter.

Economic growth will make future generations wealthier, which, by some ethical standards, reduces our obligation to make sacrifices for them. Alternative ethical standards are possible.

Any discussion of intergenerational ethics must account for the nature and sources of economic growth. Horace Mann, writing in 1845, gave an account which is essentially identical in content (though superior in style) to what you'll find in modern textbooks:

> The wealth and prosperity of Massachusetts are not owing to natural position or resources. They exist, in spite of a sterile soil and an inhospitable clime. They do not come from the earth, but from the ingenuity and frugality of the people. Their origin is good thinking, carried out into good action.

Today's textbooks attribute growth to a combination of technological progress and capital investment—in other words, the ingenuity and frugality of the people. Our descendants will reap the rewards of our ingenuity and frugality. Whether we owe them more than that is a subtle and difficult question, requiring subtle and difficult thought.

18

What My Daughter Taught Me About Money

When Cayley was eight she gave me a long lecture about what's important in life. Love is important, she explained. Money isn't.

"Well," I said, "I think there *are* a lot of people who don't care very much about money, and that's fine, but I honestly don't think you're one of them. It seems to me that you're somebody who really enjoys shopping and buying things." Cayley took up her standard exasperation pose (hands on hips, eyes squinted) and said, "*Dad!* The *reason* I like to shop and buy things is to get *rid* of my money."

Touché, Cayley. She was exactly right. Love of money and love of wealth are two quite different things. Scrooge McDuck loves money: he hoards it in a safe, where he can bathe in it every night. Richie Rich's dad enjoys his wealth as much as McDuck does, but he enjoys it in the form of mansions and artwork and servants rather than in the form of money. Cayley wants to be like Mr. Rich.

Of course Cayley has a right to her preferences, but it's worth pointing out that if she wants to be a good neighbor, she'd do well to emulate Scrooge McDuck rather than the Riches. When Richie and his dad build a mansion, they use bricks, mortar, and cement that might otherwise have become part of a hospital, a community center or a housing development.[1] They hire masons, carpenters, and electricians who might otherwise have been employed building roads, shopping centers, or—with a little retraining—automobiles. The food served at the Rich's extravagant feasts is food that nobody but the Riches and their guests can eat; the fuel burned by their private jets is made from oil that will never heat their neighbors' houses.

But when Scrooge bathes in his dollar bills, the only thing he keeps from his neighbors is a lot of cheap paper. As long as he hoards his money instead of spending it, there are more bricks and mortar, more ready workmen, more food, and more fuel for Scrooge's neighbors to enjoy.

There are some who get this exactly backward: They believe that lavish spending spreads prosperity, while a miser is a burden to the community. Cayley is too sophisticated to be taken in by those fallacies. She knows that money's not important; it's the things you *buy* with money that are important. The less Scrooge buys, the more his neighbors can buy; the more his neighbors can buy, the happier they'll be.

---

1. Or perhaps the bricks themselves are produced only in response to the order from the Riches; then the bricks are produced from labor and raw materials that had alternative uses, so the point still stands: when the Riches have more, their neighbors have less.

But if Scrooge refuses to circulate his money, how can the neighbors *afford* all that stuff? Here's the answer: By taking money out of circulation, Scrooge causes prices to drop, which makes everyone else's money go further—in fact just enough further so that they can afford to buy all the luxuries that Scrooge forgoes.

The Riches will trade you *their* money in exchange for goods and services. Scrooge, by keeping prices down, will raise the value of *your* money in exchange for nothing at all. I like Scrooge's deal better.

The Rich family's many servants don't see it that way; they know they owe their jobs and their high salaries to Richie's dad's extravagance. But Cayley sees the bigger picture: if the highly paid Rich servants can buy more, then somebody else must buy less. When Richie's personal butler gets a raise, he can claim a bigger piece of the communal pie—but the pie itself is no bigger than before.[2]

Scrooge, by contrast, continues to do his neighbors a great favor by keeping his money in the vault. If he ever has a change of heart and decides to start spending more, it will be a sad day in Duckburg. When Scrooge buys ten avocados, the laws of arithmetic dictate that some Duckburg resident must buy ten fewer avocados—or perhaps ten residents buy one fewer avocado each. The laws of economics spell out the details: Scrooge's purchase bids up the *price* of avocados until somebody somewhere decides to buy fewer of them.

A rising avocado price has three effects: Avocado lovers mourn, avocado growers celebrate, and ducks with money

2. The pie can grow, and frequently does, but growth requires some productive activity. Spending money is not a productive activity.

in their pockets see its value eaten away by avocado-driven inflation. In terms of the general prosperity of Duckburg, the second effect cancels the first, but the third remains. The net loss to moneyholders is equal in value to the ten avocados that Scrooge consumes.

Even if Scrooge *gave away* all his money, he couldn't make his neighbors (on average) any richer. Those who got the money would be richer; but they, unlike the atypically miserly Scrooge, would try to spend it. That would bid up prices, and then the average duck would be no richer than before.

That means it's impossible for Scrooge to give away wealth (as opposed to money). And the reason for that is simple: He's already traded all his wealth for a vault full of money. There's nothing left to give away.

In that sense, Scrooge the miser is a great philanthropist, the likes of which will never be seen in the Rich family. Not that there's anything reprehensible about the Rich family lifestyle. Presumably, Richie's dad did something worthwhile to *create* all that wealth. It's his right to spend it however he wants. But Scrooge, unlike Rich, did something extraordinary: He first created vast wealth and then laid claim to none of it.

Because she studies comic books instead of, say, the *Wall Street Journal,* Cayley has a deeper understanding of monetary economics than, say, the average member of the Concord Coalition. She understands, as so many editorial writers do not, that foreign citizens who hoard U.S. dollars are doing Americans a great favor. Sending paper money to Japan and getting a Toyota in exchange is just like sending a long letter to the North Pole and gettng everything you want for Christmas. As long as someone in Japan wants to hold that money, your Toyota is essentially free. It's not free to *you* of course, but it's free to Americans more generally: When Toyota accepts your dollars and takes them out of circulation, the prices of American goods fall, giving your neighbors a windfall equal to what you paid for your car.

Admittedly, prices get bid down only imperceptibly, and the benefits to each of your neighbors were correspondingly imperceptible. But an imperceptible amount times 250,000,000 Americans works out to equal the price of a Toyota. The final accounting: You spent $20,000, your neighbors got a windfall of $20,000, and you got your Toyota. The nation as a whole is one Toyota richer.

Of course, it's a fair bet that our Japanese trading partners will eventually want to spend those dollars they've been hoarding, at which point our windfall goes away. But the longer they hold the money—the longer they act like Scrooge McDuck–the longer we get to enjoy the windfall. When they start buying our goods—turning into something more like the Rich family—the party's over.

That of course is exactly the opposite of the conventional adult wisdom, according to which the road to prosperity is a trading partner who demands valuable resources and the road to ruin is a trading partner who will accept a vault full of paper. That conventional wisdom derives precisely from a confusion between money and wealth. If you make that mistake around Cayley, her eyes will squint up.

19

What My Daughter Taught Me About Trade

ONE OF CAYLEY'S FIRST GRADE CLASSmates had a guinea pig, and that guinea pig had babies. The babies were brought into school to be claimed. Multiple claims to a given guinea pig were adjudicated by the teacher, who tried to account both for strengths of preference among the children and the long-term best interests of the guinea pigs.

Cayley got lucky. Nobody else liked her favorite guinea pig, so she won it by default. That night I told her that she'd just rediscovered a key principle of classical economics: *It pays to be different*. If the things you like are unpopular, you can buy them cheap. If the things you want to get rid of are popular, you can sell them dear.

It pays to be different not just in your tastes, but also in your talents. If half the class plays clarinet, the lone tuba player has the best chance of making it into the orchestra.

That's why there's so much to be gained from trading across international boundaries. It's not just that you get a lot of new trading partners; it's that you get a lot of new trading partners who are very *different* from you. If Honda made cars exactly the same way Ford makes cars, Americans wouldn't really care whether they were allowed to buy Hondas or forced to buy Fords. It's the *difference* between an American car and a Japanese car that makes the Japanese car a valuable option.

American corporate executives drool at the prospect of serving a billion new customers in China. But when they focus on the *size* of that Chinese market, they are missing an important point: It's not just that there are so many Chinese but that the Chinese are so different. If Chinese animators were as good as Disney's animators, Disney would have no market in China. The great opportunity is created by the fact that Americans produce blockbuster movies more efficiently than Chinese, and Chinese produce silk shirts more efficiently than Americans.

That's also why, even though all parties benefit from international trade, it's the small countries that benefit most. There are significant differences between the average U.S. citizen and the average Mexican. When trade agreements make it easier for people on both sides of the border to exploit those differences, the combined North American market is dominated by the more numerous U.S. citizens. That's very good news for Mexicans: They're now trading in a market where they're very different from the average trader.

Take an example: Suppose that without international trade, coffee sells in Mexico for $3 a pound and in the United States for $7 a pound. Now if we suddenly open the border to create a single North American market in coffee, the price will settle somewhere between $3 and $7. From the Mexican point of view, that's a price increase, and hence an opportunity to profit by selling coffee. To U.S. citizens, it's a price decrease, and hence an opportunity to buy coffee at a bargain. The average American and the average Mexican both gain.

But who gains the most? Because the United States dominates the market, the new price will probably be much closer to $7 than to $3. That means that Mexicans get a big profit opportunity, while those in the United States get only a small bargain. The Mexican's great good fortune is that he is farther from the North American average than his northern neighbor—and the reason he is farther from the average is because he has fewer countrymen.

The great eighteenth century economist Adam Smith stressed that trade benefits people by letting them specialize. In other words, if my wife and I each want to make a dozen frosted cupcakes, it makes sense for one of us to bake a double batch of cupcakes while the other prepares a double batch of frosting. That's so even if we're both equally good at baking and both equally good at frosting. The basic principle is that doing something twice is often less than twice as hard as doing something once.

But the great nineteenth century economist David Ricardo stressed that the advantages of trade are magnified by differences between the trading partners. If I'm a better baker than my wife and she's a better froster than me, our trade becomes even more rewarding.[1]

Ricardo's emphasis on differences is the standard stuff of economics textbooks, and I was glad to be able to share it with my daughter on the occasion of her new guinea pig. She knew she'd gotten her favorite animal because it was nobody else's favorite; on this very day, she'd seen that it pays to be different.

To drive that point home, I asked her whether she'd rather trade pogs[2] with a kid whose tastes are similar to hers or a kid whose tastes are very different. That's a translation into kid-talk of a question that I often ask on college exams. Cayley got the wrong answer by choosing the trading partner who resembles her. But, unlike a lot of my students, she got the wrong answer for interesting reasons.

First, she explained that there's no challenge in dealing with somebody who agrees to every trade you propose. In pog trading, it seems, all the fun comes from identifying and exploiting slight (and rare) differences of opinion. When Cayley discovers, contrary to all expectation, that

---

1. Actually, Ricardo's insight was more profound than that. Even if I am both a better baker *and* a better froster than my wife, I still gain by trading with her. By letting her do the frosting (at which I am only slightly better), I free myself to do more baking (at which I am much better). In general, whenever people—or countries—have different abilities, those differences create mutually beneficial trade opportunities—even when one party is better than the other at *everything.*

2. For those who are either too old or too young to recognize the word "pog," a pog is a small cardboard disk with a design or a picture of some hero of popular culture. At the time of the incident I'm describing, a frenzy of pog trading had converted elementary school playgrounds around the country into impromptu exchange floors. More recently, the furor seems to have abated.

her friend Jessica is willing to part with the Lisa Simpson pog that Cayley covets, both girls get a rush of exhilaration. If Cayley had traded instead with Samantha, who is known to hate everything that Cayley likes, there would be more good trades but no wonderful surprises.

That was a new insight for me, but one that I think is unlikely to have important consequences beyond the pog market. It's hard to imagine, for example, that serious shoppers would choose the most expensive grocery store just for the thrill of finding an occasional bargain, while eschewing the discount store for the sole reason that discounts are no fun when they're too easy to come by.

But as we continued our discussion, Cayley forced me to confront two further issues that I think *are* important in trade theory, even though they're not standard textbook fare (at least not in the sophomore level classes that I usually teach).

First, she argued (though not exactly in this language) that it's useful to have a trading partner who can accurately anticipate your demands. Maybe Samantha has no use for Lisa Simpson pogs and would happily sell them cheap. But if Samantha is sufficiently different from Cayley, it might never occur to her that Lisa Simpson pogs have any value, so she might not bother to bring them to the table. On a grander scale, this means that it can be difficult to carry on trade between vastly different cultures because, for example, American manufacturers have difficulty anticipating the preferences of African villagers.

Second, she argued that Samantha, like all of her friends, is primarily a pog *collector,* and only secondarily a pog *trader.* That's important, because it means that Samantha tends to be carrying the pogs Samantha likes to collect, rather than the pogs she thinks Cayley will want to buy. But the pogs that Samantha likes to collect have little appeal to Cayley, so Samantha has very little to offer her.

That analysis flies in the face of what's in the textbooks. The textbooks assume that your trading partner will show up trying to sell the things that *you* like, rather than the things that *he* likes. Under that assumption (which I think is basically correct most of the time), there's no advantage to having a partner who shares your preferences. But in the special case of a collector, that assumption is turned on its head, because the collector actively enjoys carrying merchandise that reflects his own preferences. In that case, you might want to find a partner who likes pretty much the same things you do.

Cayley was right—but only up to a point. I collect books of modern poetry, and I'd certainly rather swap books with another poetry lover than with, say, a collector of Cliff's Notes. In other words, I want a trading partner who is a lot like I am. But I'd never want to swap books with a poetry lover who is *exactly* like I am. We'd both have identical collections and we'd both have the same special favorites. We'd both agree that a first edition of Dylan Thomas is worth exactly three John Berrymans. It would be hopeless for us to find a trade we could both agree to.[3] So it still pays to be at least a *bit* different.

---

3. Actually, it's not *necessarily* hopeless: If we each have one Thomas and one Berryman, and if for some reason we each want above all to have two identical books, then there's a gain from trade: I walk off with two Thomases and my friend walks off with two Berrymans, or vice versa. The general rule is that identical people *who value variety* cannot gain from trade.

My daughter's experiences in the pog market hardly threaten to overturn the foundations of international trade theory, and they don't refute Ricardo's fundamental insight that as a general rule, differences are the key to successful trading. But she did identify some interesting exceptions to that general rule. Those exceptions are sufficiently subtle that fully incorporating them into a formal economic model might be a substantial research project for a graduate student; they are sufficiently interesting that such a project might be worthwhile. When you listen carefully, kids do indeed say the darndest things.

20

Advice to an Economist's Daughter

There's no use trying to succeed at something unless you love what you're doing. You'll always be competing against people who *do* love what they're doing, and it's unlikely you'll muster enough energy to compete successfully unless you love your work as much as they do.

If you're not making mistakes, you're not taking enough risks. If you never fall off your bicycle, you're not having enough fun. If you never miss your plane, you're spending too much time in airports.

Beware of those who tell you to eat natural food because it's healthy. Have these people never heard of toadstools?

The truth is that "natural" foods are derived from creatures who have survived natural selection, where it's an advantage to be deadly. "Artificial" foods are designed to survive in the marketplace, where it's an advantage to be nourishing.

Beware of those who pontificate about "the majesty of the law."

We live in New York State, where they've outlawed those little clicky things on the gas pumps—the ones you use to keep the gas flowing while you walk around to check your oil. At some moment in the past, some New York State legislator must have gathered some colleagues around him and said "We've got to do something about those little clicky things," and they all nodded sagely. That's the majesty of the law.

Don't mistake a *hard* bargainer for a *good* bargainer. To bargain hard in the final stages, you must risk bringing down the whole deal. Who's most willing to take such risks? Those who gave away too much in the early stages, that's who. The hardest bargainers at the end are those who were the worst bargainers at the beginning.

Take charge of your life. Rely on professionals for their expertise, not for their opinions about what you should value.

No doctor is qualified to prescribe treatments for your medical problems. Only you can know what risks you're willing to accept and what sacrifices you're willing to make for various aspects of your health. Doctors can help you understand the costs and benefits of various treatments, but only you can weigh those costs and benefits against each other. Allowing a doctor to choose your medication is like allowing a waiter to choose your dinner entree.

Diversify, in your investment strategy and in life generally.

A lot of people are less diversified than they think they are. They own stocks in companies that are influential in their hometowns. That's almost always a mistake: If the company falls on bad times, both your stocks *and* your real estate will suffer.

Cayley, if you are ever in the position to sell water for $7 a gallon I want you to charge $7 a gallon and not a penny less. That's not because I want you to make a lot of money—I have a feeling you'll be doing pretty well in some more stable career anyway. It's because it's your social responsibility to get that water to those who need it most desperately, and if you charge less than the market will bear then the wrong people will claim the water.

When I was a child, I once saw a group of other children trying to climb a few feet up a telephone pole. They weren't getting very far, and they obviously weren't *going* to get very far, but they were having a lot of fun trying.

After a few minutes, a woman who lived a few houses away came out of her house and chased the children away.

That night, I was talking to my older cousin, who must have been about sixteen years old at the time. I asked him why the woman chased the children away. I thought maybe there was some danger I didn't know about.

The answer he gave me is one of the most vivid memories of my childhood. He shrugged and said, "Some people just can't stand to see other people having a good time."

That, I think, goes a long way toward explaining why our government is so large, why our taxes are so high, and why our lives are so regulated. Some people just can't stand to see other people having a good time. Never underestimate the power of that force.

Surf the Internet. I'd much rather have you getting your pornography from cyberspace than by rummaging around your parents' bedroom.

In fact, I'm glad the net makes it easy for you to get ahold of things that other people would prefer you not to get ahold of. Family values crusader Donna Rice[1] complains that "any child with a computer can access vile pornography in a matter of seconds. And once they have seen it, it can never be erased from their minds." You betcha, Donna. The Internet is the natural enemy of those who are out to erase other people's minds.

Let's be honest—access to pornography is not part of the *cost* of the Internet; it's one of the *benefits*. The whole *purpose* of the Internet is to facilitate communication and to thwart those who would hamper the free exchange of information.

---

1. If you're a reader old enough to remember Gary Hart and the *Monkey Business*, the answer to your question is: Yes, *that* Donna Rice.

Don't take summer jobs while you're still in school, unless you've exhausted every opportunity to borrow. It's crazy to work when you're young and unskilled; the same amount of effort a few years later will be far more rewarding. Spend your student years studying; if you learn something at age 16 instead of 26, you'll have an additional ten years of knowing it.

When you're choosing a college, try this thought experiment: Imagine that you've walked into a living room where a small circle of people is talking animatedly and excitedly while several others sit quietly on the sidelines. If you wanted to know what the conversation was about, who would you prefer to ask? If you think the partcipants would give you a more accurate and enticing answer than the observers, then you should go to a university where you're going to be taught by active researchers.

A good way to decide whether someone's values are attractive is by looking at them in a mirror. When somebody tells you that it's immoral for sellers to seek high prices, ask him whether it's immoral for buyers to seek low prices.

The greatest rewards come not to those who perform necessary tasks, but to those who figure out which tasks are necessary and then perform them.

Never stop exploring life's options, even if you end up right where you started. Home is a lot sweeter once you've been around the basepaths.

Don't make the mistake of marrying the best possible husband, any more than you would make the mistake of buying the best possible car. They're both likely to cost more than they're worth to you.

Your ideal mate is probably close to ideal for a lot of other people, too. That means you'll have to make concessions to win him and concessions to keep him—on every issue from how many children you'll have to who's cooking dinner tonight. A perfect husband is a costly extravagance. Most costly extravagances turn out to be mistakes.

Write your own marriage contract (together with your fiancé of course). Most people don't, which was an ongoing source of dismay to late Nobel-prize winning economist George Stigler. He maintained that the grand institution of matrimony is demeaned by those who can't be bothered to negotiate its details.

Without a prenuptial contract, you will be governed by marital and community property laws that are an abomination and an insult to human dignity. The laws effectively give your spouse the right to levy a 50% tax on your savings. But they don't allow a tax on any other activity, like earning and spending, or enjoying leisure time. If you spend an hour lying by the poolside, the law says that's fine; you've not been derelict in any duty. But if you spend the same hour working to accumulate savings, you suddenly acquire a duty to share those savings with your spouse. That's asymmetric, and it's profoundly wrong.

If you have an opportunity to earn $10, that opportunity either does or does not create a moral obligation to pay something to your spouse. If that obligation exists, how can you be completely absolved of it by choosing to ignore the opportunity? If the obligation does not exist, then marital property is theft.

Marital property is abhorrent for exactly the same reasons that the progressive income tax is abhorrent. First, it says that your moral responsibilities can change as a result of choices you make, even when those choices are morally irrelevant. And second, it says that your moral responsibilities are unlimited; there never comes a point when you have fulfilled your duty honorably and are discharged from further responsibility. There is no cap on marital property.

If you're unimpressed by philosophical niceties, then consider this: People who lay claim to other people's income are in general not very appealing. People who lay claim to *your* income are unsuitable as house guests, let alone life partners.

When you're married and dividing the housework, keep this principle in mind: If you and your husband have similar skills, there's nothing to be gained from sharing housework. You're just reassigning tasks from one person to someone else who does them equally well. If you want to be efficient, you'll do better by specializing—one in housework and the other in the marketplace.

But if you and your husband have very *different* skills, it makes sense to share the housework, so that all of those skills can be brought to bear.

Feminists and male chauvinists both have this backward. Feminists say that because men and women are very similar, they should share the housework. That's wrong; if men and women are similar, each of them should choose a specialty and stick to it. Male chauvinists say that because men and women are very different, women should specialize in housework. That's also wrong; the more differences there are, the stronger is the case for sharing tasks.

Of course, you might also want to share tasks for other reasons, like togetherness—or because a given person can only do so much housework before needing to do something else or go crazy.

Ponder philosophy. It matters. Follow logic wherever it leads you. Take fables seriously; they strip away irrelevant detail and reveal great truths. Calculate. If your ideas can't be translated sensibly into mathematics, there's something wrong with them.

Never forget that there are a lot of people who know a lot more than you do about a lot of things that are important. Listen carefully to what they have to say.

Defer immediately to a good argument. But never defer to mere authority. If you have good teachers, they will encourage you.

I hope you read this book someday. When you publish your rebuttal, I'll be first in line for an autographed copy.

Appendix: Further Reading

Here is a list of the published sources that I referred to in the chapters of this book.

What Cayley Knows. James Ingram's fable appears in his book *International Economic Problems,* published by John Wiley and Sons in 1966, reprinted in 1970, and issued in paperback in 1978.

Authority. The data on how education majors stack up against college students generally are taken from a paper on "Who Chooses to Teach (and Why)?" by Eric Hanushek and Rick Pace, in the *Economics of Education Review,* 1995. John Lott's paper on the public provision of education appeared in the *Journal of Law and Economics,* April 1990. James Kahn's paper on "A Hobbesian Model of Government" has not yet appeared in print. I first learned about the Mafia's tax on the New York construction industry from *Goombata* by J. Cummings and E. Volkman, published by Little Brown in 1992.

What Life Has to Offer. Dylan Thomas's remarks on the sound of poetry are from a hard-to-find essay called "Notes on the Art of Poetry," consisting of Thomas's responses to written questions submitted by a young student. The essay appears in the volume *A Garland for Dylan Thomas,* published in 1963 by Clarke and Way. Whittaker Chambers's *Letter to My Children* appears as the preface to his autobiography *Witness,* first published in 1952 by Random House and currently in print as a paperback from Regnery.

Cultural Biases. The book referred to in the first paragraph was written by a man named George F. Will. Jeff Green of Hutchinson Technology suggested the survey question about parental influence on children's values. The Princeton economists who have challenged the conventional wisdom about the minimum wage are David Card and Alan Krueger; their book *Myth and Measurement: The New Economics of the Minimum Wage* was published by the Princeton University Press in 1995.

Fairness I: The Grandfather Fallacy. For some of the history of the idea of compensated emancipation, see David Herbert Donald's excellent biography *Lincoln,* published in 1995 by Simon & Schuster.

Fairness II: The Symmetry Principle. Parts of this chapter were heavily inspired by a 1996 address to the Philadelphia Society by the legal scholar Michael Krauss. Krauss's themes were the moral basis for tort law and the lamentable erosion of that moral basis; while tort law used to be based on simple moral principles that everyone could understand (like "don't hit people"), it now serves as a mechanism for enforcing public policies that have no clear moral underpinnings (like "hire the handicapped"). In other words, it used to be that an action had to be *wrong* to be tortious, whereas now it need only violate some perceived public purpose—and the old way was better. In this chapter, I've tried to emphasize that a law which is based on clear moral principles cannot impose more responsibility on one citizen than on another; that is, it must satisfy the symmetry principle. I'm not entirely sure whether Professor Krauss would be pleased with that formulation, but I do owe him a great intellectual debt.

The Perfect Tax. The trait tax (along with its justification) is the invention of my colleague Mark Bils. Mark is also the proud author of the defense of affirmative action which I characterized in the chapter as "pathetic."

The Perfect Tax, Deconstructed. George Bernard Shaw's thoughts on income redistribution (and every other topic you might imagine) are recorded in his *Intelligent Woman's Guide to Socialism, Capitalism, Sovietism, and Fascism,* published in 1928 by Brentano's.

Bequests. For evidence that estates are usually divided equally among children, see the essay by Paul Menchik in the *Quarterly Journal of Economics* (1980). For a bit of counterevidence, see the essay by Nigel Tomes in the *Journal of Political Economy* (1981). The discussion of schooling versus bequests as vehicles for redistributing income across children is based on an essay reprinted in Gary Becker's *Treatise* *on the Family,* published by the Harvard University Press (1991). Becker is also the source for the observation that parental instincts to redistribute can undercut the effects of programs like Head Start. The effects of family size and birth order were reported by my colleague Eric Hanushek in the *Journal of Political Economy* in 1992; his essay is called "Tradeoffs Between Child Quantity and Quality." For evidence that parents with bequeathable wealth get more visits from their children than parents with an equal amount of non-bequeathable wealth, see the article by Douglas Bernheim, Andrei Shleifer, and Lawrence Summers in the *Journal of Political Economy* (1985).

After this chapter was written, I learned about the research of Professor Thomas Dunn at Syracuse University. Professor Dunn's research supports the hypothesis that parents divide their bequests equally without regard to the incomes of their children (though gifts during life are distributed far less equally).

People Wanted. Professor Michael Kremer's provocatively titled essay "Population Growth and Technological Change: One Million B.C. to 1900" appeared in the *Quarterly Journal of Economics* in 1993. The two economists at the Federal Reserve Bank of Richmond are Marvin Goodfriend and J. McDermott; their essay on "Early Development" appeared in the *American Economic Review* in 1995. The observation that a crime which prevents its victims from existing is a victimless crime is from Wilfred Beckerman's excellent and provcative book *Through Green-Colored Glasses* (published by Cato in 1996), and attributed there to the philosopher Derek Parfit. I enthusiastically recommend Peter Bauer's book *The Development Frontier: Essays in Applied Economics,* published by Harvard University Press in 1991.

The Third R. Required readings for anyone with a serious interest in education are Horace Mann's *Lectures on Education,* delivered annually under the auspices of the Boston Board of Education and published as a collection by the Board in 1845.

The Arithmetic of Discrimination. The research by Derek Neal and William Johnson appeared in the *Journal of Political Economy* in 1996. The Horace Mann quote is again from his *Lectures on Education.*

Advice to an Economist's Daughter. George Stigler's observations on the sanctity of marriage appear in his *Memoirs of an Unregulated Economist,* published by Basic Books in 1988. The observations on how housework should be divided are from Gary Becker's *Treatise on the Family.*

Index